ROBE

Minorcan Gumbo
FOR THE SOUL

A St. Augustine, Florida Story

outskirts press

Minorcan Gumbo for the Soul
A St. Augustine, Florida Story
All Rights Reserved.
Copyright © 2018 Robert P. Jones
v2.0

The opinions expressed in this manuscript are solely the opinions of the author and do not represent the opinions or thoughts of the publisher. The author has represented and warranted full ownership and/or legal right to publish all the materials in this book.

This book may not be reproduced, transmitted, or stored in whole or in part by any means, including graphic, electronic, or mechanical without the express written consent of the publisher except in the case of brief quotations embodied in critical articles and reviews.

Outskirts Press, Inc.
http://www.outskirtspress.com

ISBN: 978-1-4787-9648-0

Cover Photo © 2018 thinkstockphotos.com. All rights reserved - used with permission.

Outskirts Press and the "OP" logo are trademarks belonging to Outskirts Press, Inc.

PRINTED IN THE UNITED STATES OF AMERICA

Contents

Teddy 1

Living at the Foot of the Bridge 5

A Taste of Shrimp That Lasts a Lifetime 32

Me and Gary Cooper 36

An Evening to Remember 44

A God Thing in Philadelphia 49

Sonny Burchfield 52

Graduation Day USMC Training Depot,
Parris Island, South Carolina 60

Bobby, Mike, Glenn, and Saint Christopher 64

The Copper-Topped Coffee Table and Its People 71

The Inheritance 82

The Chairs 89

Bucky Powers 98

Bobby Jones' First Prom 113

A Day Remembered In My Trade 116

A Saturday in Remembrance of My Mother 124

Fishing with Grandson Mike Jones 128

The Fishing Trip from Hell 133

My Uncle Lester 143

A Name on a Monument in St. Augustine 150

"I Think They Will" 157

He really is in Charge 162

A Moment of Spiritual Enchantment 166

Ever Think You Are in Charge? 169

My Special Board of Memories 174

Speaking of My Mortality 176

Writing and publishing a novel was an elusive dream I chased all my adult life. I finally accepted the reality at 84 years of age that if I have any writing skill at all, it is in the genre of short stories. I regret not being disciplined enough to spend the daily hours necessary to master the craft of writing. Writing is a grand craft. It requires time-tested rules to follow out of respect for your readers.

Everyone has a narrative. Not everyone wishes to share theirs for myriad reasons, but many feel a burning desire to share experiences with their fellow travelers on life's short journey.

I was encouraged to keep writing stories by Margo C. Pope, an outstanding citizen of St. Augustine, Florida. Her father, Coach Red Cox, was one of my heroes when I played sports at Francis Field and at St. Joseph's Academy. Margo was editorial page editor of the *St. Augustine Record* during a portion of her twenty-four years of service to the community. She was one of the leaders helping to restore the War Memorial in the St. Augustine Plaza. Thank you, Margo, for helping a boy from Vilano Beach.

I hope you enjoy the stories. The journey has been wonderful, eclectic and blessed with a feeling of hope and joy. Still being very much in love with the lady I married on May 28, 1955 makes this journey a true gift. Thank you, Malinda Usina Jones.

Teddy

WE OWNED AN Eskimo Spitz named Teddy when I was eight years old. He had snow white fur, but it was always dirty because he went everywhere I was allowed to go. He had a black tongue and licked me every chance he got. I didn't mind that at all!

The Jones family lived in St. Augustine, Florida, at 146 Cunningham Avenue in a yellow frame house with a long front porch, tin roof, and partially dirt front yard. The house was high enough off the ground that us kids could crawl under it, find spider webs to wrap around sticks, and then go to a doodle bug hole and chant; "Doodle bug, doodle bug, won't you come out?" The doodle bugs were attracted to the spider webs and usually crawled slowly out of their dirt holes. We gently picked them up with our dirty little fingers and put them in glass jars with punched air holes in the tin caps. I don't remember whether we experimented with the doodle bugs, but we kept them alive and later let them go.

Our little world was two blocks in any direction. Aunt

MINORCAN GUMBO FOR THE SOUL

Pat's in-laws, Freddie and May Shugart, lived directly across the street. Aunt Pat and Uncle Lloyd lived in a garage apartment down a gravel lane next to the Shugarts. Our next door neighbors to the north were the Carcabas. Also to the north were the Bazemores and the McClendons.

The Andreu family lived around the corner three or four houses from the Florida East Coast railroad tracks. Walter Andreu was my best friend. Albert Andreu and my brother, Richard, were best buds. There were lots of kids at the Andreu house. Walter's mother, who was a large woman, was from New York. She had the loudest voice in the world. Walter's daddy, Joe, was an outstanding master carpenter about half the size of his wife and as quiet as a mouse.

Grandfather Brinson, who was blind and lived with us, had retired from the Florida East Coast railroad. He was an engineer who brought back one of the last passenger trains from Key West to Miami during the hurricane that killed thousands.

He received a pension from the railroad. Each month when his check came, he cashed it and gave Richard and me a half-dollar, a quarter, a dime, a nickel, and a penny. We were richer than any other kid in this North City neighborhood on that day. As soon as our allowance was in hand, Richard, Teddy, and I would race to Russell's drive-in to buy a hamburger, French fries, and a cold bottle of Coke.

Russell's Bar B Que was constructed of concrete and wood. It was painted black and white and was often

TEDDY

referred to by the locals, who said, "Meet you at the Black and White." Teddy would patiently sit under the outside stools we sat on until we finished every last bite of the best hamburger in the world. To this day, I have never tasted a hamburger as good as Russell Allen's, and I have tried them all over the world.

Russell's was on San Marco Avenue, which was also US 1, the only road that ran through St. Augustine, except for a portion of Highway A1A. If you were coming from the north or south you had to travel on San Marco Avenue to go through St. Augustine.

One afternoon, I was at Russell's when I heard the screech of brakes and a loud horn blaring. I froze in place, laid the hamburger down on the counter and turned toward San Marco Avenue. I didn't see the Greyhound bus hit Teddy, but I knew something was wrong when the bus stopped and Teddy was nowhere in sight. I somehow made it across the street to find Teddy lying there still and quiet. I knelt down, picked him up, and remember someone saying how sorry they were that my dog was hurt.

Thinking back on that event, it had to be the first time I felt heartbreak. I remember tears streaming down my dirty face. I think someone took Teddy from my arms and walked me home to Momma. I have never loved another pet the way I loved Teddy.

I tell this story for anyone who has lost a pet. Just as I remember the gentleness and personality of Teddy with joy, I know you feel the same way about your pet.

Each time I look at a picture of Teddy, I am mentally transported to San Marco Avenue. I see a shirtless boy in faded dungarees who hated to wear shoes, loved to climb trees in the "Big Woods," loved to play baseball at St. Agnes dirt field, and throw "light rocks" along the railroad tracks into the San Sebastian River while waiting for a train to come along and run over a penny I put on the tracks.

To my wonderful children, grandchildren and great-grandchildren: it is okay to lose a pet you love because you can bring that beloved pet back to life anytime you wish through your memories. It's okay to shed a tear every now and then because these extraordinary tears can drive away the cobwebs from your mind. It also helps you become more aware of the good things in your life.

Teddy with my uncle, Sergeant Lester Brinson KIA

Living at the Foot of the Bridge

A HAPPY POINT in my life began in the summer of 1948. My mother, Mary Frances Brinson Jones, and her three children (me at age 14, Richard 10, and Lesta Ann 4), moved into a small white board and batten cabin at P.J. Manucy's Riverside Fish Camp on Vilano Beach, Florida. The cabin was twelve feet wide and sixteen feet long, but seemed much bigger at the time.

We had moved from Miami in 1946 and lived at Iva and Lawson Cowart's farm until Vilano Beach became our home. In today's jargon, we were homeless until we moved into the cabin. Even so, during those four years, we were sheltered by other families; we had food and clothing, and never slept on the street. Our Guardian Angels watched over us then and still do.

The Vilano Beach Bridge Was Special

An old wooden bascule bridge separated folks on Vilano Beach from folks in St. Augustine. Vilano Beach

MINORCAN GUMBO FOR THE SOUL

residents often believed they were separated physically, culturally, and economically from St. Augustine; and they were okay with that. As a teenager, I had no philosophy like that. I liked everyone, especially girls.

The bridge had two narrow lanes constructed of rough-hewn wooden planks covered with a concoction of asphalt and tar. There were discernible openings between some of the planks wide enough to see the river below. The tires on the heavy passenger cars and trucks of the 1940s played a unique syncopated clackety clack clackety clack on the timbers that held up the cars and trucks driving across what to me was an ancient bridge. To my big ears, it sounded like the 4x12 inch planks would break loose and jump off their support beams, but none ever did. The Florida State Road Department architects must have specified huge steel nails and bolts to keep the heavy planks in place from so much daily wear and tear at a time when there were probably not any enforced weight restrictions.

There was a bridge-tender whose only job seemed to be raising and lowering the cantankerous old drawbridge when tall boats signaled him to do so. It was obvious to the people driving across the bridge every day that workers from the State Road Department were always busy maintaining the rusty, often-malfunctioning, machinery used to raise and lower the draw.

Heavy black and white guardrails with flashing red

lights dropped to a horizontal position before the draw was raised, warning traffic in both directions to stop. The only barrier beyond the guardrail was the raised steel draw. If vehicles failed to stop at the flashing guardrail, they slammed head-on into the elevated metal shield. There, they would stop suddenly. Several times drivers heading back to St. Augustine after a raucous party at Surfside Casino learned a hard lesson. I don't recall any deaths, but I heard there were plenty of broken bones and noses.

All we young studs thought that being a bridge-tender had to be the best job possible. All you had to do was operate the bridge machinery when a boat was ready to pass under. Then, all you did the rest of the time was sit in the old broken-down leather chair and read the St. Augustine Record, listen to WFOY on the radio, or stand by the rail puffing a cigarette waiting for the next boat to blow her loud horn. As we got older, we found out that getting a bridge-tender job was a matter of high political patronage, guaranteeing a pension for the lucky employee after twenty years of service.

It was neat when Richard and I got close to the open drawbridge. We saw gleaming white yachts motoring up and down the Intercoastal Waterway from myriad destinations in South Florida and up to Maine. Lessie was too young to go on the bridge with us so she played at the house with Linda Manucy. They are still great friends and visit often.

Richard and I liked to hear the powerful engines rev up and return to full speed after slowing down to go through the draw. We could only imagine the size and horsepower of those diesel engines. The fastest boat we ever rode on was the trusty, rusty Victory II owned by Captain Francis Usina, a St. Augustine Minorcan icon. The engine on the Victory II sounded powerful enough but didn't compare with the twin diesel or gasoline engines in the big yachts that passed us by. When we had our fill of yacht watching, we sauntered down the bridge back to our cabin or ran out on the dock to watch the commercial fishermen unload their catch. I don't recall wanting to change places with the people on the yachts and sometimes wondered if they had as much fun as I was having.

The Riverside Fish Camp

P.J. Manucy, Sr. had five small cabins that he rented mostly to fishermen who drove down from Jacksonville or Georgia to spend the night so that they could be in the boat and on the river fishing before sunrise. At the end of the day, most bought beer and sandwiches at P.J., Sr's grocery store and listened to the jukebox until the store closed around midnight. Fishermen caught an assortment of speckled trout, red drum, whiting, sheepshead, flounder, and black drum. There were very few regulations for sports fishing and no armed law enforcement officers to monitor saltwater fishing activity. Fishing was fun, but there were only a few thousand sport fishermen in 1947 and 1948.

My first real job was working for P.J. Manucy, Jr. He was a hardworking man. He and his wife, Sadie, always treated me well. I had to be on the dock before sunrise making sure all the rental boats' wooden seats were wiped down and dry. P.J. paid me one dollar per day. If I hustled and helped the fishermen, they gave me a tip which added up to the dollar salary. I think I gave all the money to Mama until I got old enough to seriously notice girls. Then I kept some jingle in my own pocket.

All the rental boats were built of plywood. They were painted green on the outside, gray on the inside deck, and red lead on the bottom. Riverside Fish Camp was painted on the side in case they ever broke free from the dock. They were very seaworthy for river boats. Billy Sanchez, a heritage St. Augustine boat-builder who had an extraordinary knack for sturdy building, built these safe fishing boats capable of fishing in the sometimes calm and sometimes treacherous St. Augustine Inlet.

P.J., Jr. was a distributor for Martin Motors. Fishermen who didn't want to row could rent a 7½ hp Martin for about $5.00 a day. I sometimes flinched when a fisherman rented a motor because I had to carry it to the boat, wrestle it down a couple of slippery wooden stairs, lay it gently into the boat, jump onto the boat, clamp the outboard motor on the stern, and chain it securely to the transom so it wouldn't fall overboard.

Sunday was the hardest day of the week because all boats were rented, except when it stormed. By Sunday evening, after cleaning and sponging out all the boats and making sure they were tied properly, I never had any trouble falling asleep, nor did I feel strong enough to get into much mischief.

The Cabin

The cabin we lived in for about three years had two bedrooms with one double bed in each room. Mama and Lessie shared a bed, and Richard and I shared one. The bedrooms were on the east side of the cabin so that we got the morning sun, but it was cooler at night. There was no such thing as air conditioners, so maybe P.J. figured this out when he built them.

It had a very compact kitchen with barely enough room for a small aluminum table and four chairs. There was an icebox, sink, and kerosene stove. The bathroom had a toilet, sink, and a tub without a shower. It was on the west side at the back of the cabin. It only had cold sulphur water, so when we took a bath, we heated a pot of water on the stove and poured it into the cold, rust stained, porcelain tub. Otherwise, we went swimming, which is what I did most of the year. Mama made coffee, Kool-Aid, and tea using sulphur water that was piped into all of the cabins from an eight-inch free-flowing well. It was cold enough to crack your teeth and it took a year or so to get used to drinking city water once we left Vilano Beach.

To write there was nothing fancy or glitzy about the fish camp cabin would be the understatement of the century. We had sparse linens, utensils, chinet-type plastic plates, and just enough clothes to get by, with one change of pants a week. We had a roach problem every now and then, but we got the Flit and sprayed the house before we went to bed. God only knows what chemicals were in the can of Flit spray (probably Malathion and DDT), but whatever it was, it killed the roaches and palmetto bugs but spared us.

The icebox in the cabin was really a box where we put a big chunk of ice in the top compartment that we bought for 25 cents from the local ice man. The ice man we knew was strong and burly and used his tongs like a scalpel. The food on the bottom shelf was kept cold until all the ice melted. We kept everything covered because palmetto bugs sometimes got into the ice box, and you could hear them at night crawling on the tinfoil covering the food. If I think about that today, it still gives me the creeps. I often wondered why Noah put palmetto bugs, mosquitoes, roaches and rats on the Ark.

After we moved from Vilano Beach, it took a long time to get used to drinking coffee made with city water. I still enjoy bending down to a flowing sulphur well pipe, sometimes having to push the green stringy growth aside,

◄ MINORCAN GUMBO FOR THE SOUL

and drinking the water from cupped hands. Sulphur water smells a bit like rotten eggs to many people, but it smells like Vilano Beach and Riverside Fish Camp to me. It was cold enough straight out of the ground; it was good, and it was pure.

Old Vilano Beach

Vilano Beach in the late 1940s was sparsely developed. Highway A1A ran through it on the way to Palm Valley, Ponte Vedra, Pablo Beach, Atlantic Beach and Mayport. There wasn't much commercial activity between the Riverside Fish Camp at the foot of the bridge and Eddie's Seabreeze Restaurant located at the big left turn in the road going east toward the ocean. Haley's Court was on the north side of A1A, and sometime around this era, I think the Barancottas built an Italian restaurant on the south side of A1A.

The Carcaba family lived on Vilano Beach at the end of a long dusty road off A1A north. Every day he worked, Hubert Carcaba brought a load of "fenders and clinkers" from his job at the gas company and scattered them on top of the narrow gravel road to his house on the North River. His regular job involved burning coal to create gas used for distribution to customers, and the residue was what was called "fenders and clinkers." His son, Bill, told me on November 17, 2006, that the material his father put on the road in the 1940s is still there today and in good shape.

LIVING AT THE FOOT OF THE BRIDGE

My brother, Richard, and I never ventured as far as Carcaba Road. We didn't go anywhere we couldn't walk because we had no bikes, and Mama had no car. We couldn't make it up to Usina's Fish Camp unless some adult took us there for a special treat. Our daddy, who divorced Mama in 1944, lived in Jacksonville. He was an excellent automobile mechanic. He came down a couple of times and took us fishing at Usina's. Daddy always caught a cooler full of fish.

Captain Francis Usina and sons, Jack and Frank, kept their old St. Augustine Sightseeing Boat, Victory II, tied to their dock when they weren't out on a tour and they always treated us well. I don't know how long the Usinas have been taking tourists on tours of Matanzas Bay, but it began long before my time. They were operating the Victory II, not Victory I, when I lived at the foot of the bridge. Going to Usina's Fish Camp was very special because they had a screened-in café. They served delicious fried St. Augustine shrimp, hush puppies, local oysters, and local fish.

My world was primarily Riverside Fish Camp from the bridge eastward to the corner of A1A where Eddie Rehling's Seabreeze restaurant was located. We had full run of the vacant land south, east, and north of the fish camp. There were no houses from the inlet around to the fish camp, so we easily walked at the edge of North River all the way to the inlet. However, I recall Mama telling us that if she ever heard of us swimming in the inlet, she would tan our butts. We believed her and never had the urge to test her resolve.

We often ran to the jetties at the inlet to watch people catch sheepshead using fiddler crabs as bait on long bamboo poles. We watched fishermen catch mullet with cast nets and helped them gather up the fish if they let us. Going to the jetties was very special to me as a kid and was also special in 2017 as an octogenarian.

The river frontage south of Highway A1A on Vilano Beach where we lived is nothing but a memory now. Houses are being built to the north of the Riverside Fish Camp on land that is so pristine and important to the ecology of North River. The upscale Porpoise Point subdivision developed all the land available. Another pristine riverfront area was lost to the public at large for the benefit of a few. Big homes and bigger egos have taken access to the beach away from the citizens. No estuary should ever be destroyed in the name of progress because it is actually regressing. As the old English adage goes, "They hang the thief who steals the goose and removes it from the commons, but the greater thief they turn loose who steals the commons from the goose." When estuaries are filled, that is stealing the commons from the people. Shame on us.

Hiking for Kerosene

One of the toughest chores we had was when the well-worn heater in the cabin ran out of kerosene. Richard and I had to hike to the Seabreeze Restaurant because they sold the only kerosene on Vilano Beach.

We used a broomstick handle to carry the five-gallon can of kerosene back to the cabin. It was easy walking to get the kerosene. I carried the empty can while Richard carried the broomstick. After paying Eddie Rehling and watching him fill the can, we put the broomstick through the top handle, lifted the heavy can, and began our long walk back to the cabin.

The trip back seemed three times longer. Richard usually had to rest a few times because he was younger, but I didn't mind taking a break myself. The can probably didn't weigh more than about 40 pounds, but it seemed like 140 by the time we made it to the door of the cabin.

Until Mama was sure I could do it without blowing up the cabin, she was the only one who could light the heater. The way those old kerosene heaters worked was to pour about one gallon into the holding tank and open up a little soot-covered window near the bottom of the heater to expose the wick. When enough kerosene was on the wick, Mama turned a knob to raise it a little more and lit it with a match. She increased the heat by raising the wick and lowered the heat by turning the wick down.

When we could afford kerosene, the cabin was toasty

warm. When no alimony check arrived or there was no money to buy the kerosene, during cold nights we slept bundled up like Eskimos. We slept without heat many, many times when Daddy didn't send the alimony check of $10 per week. It was supposed to be $40 per week under the divorce agreement of November, 1944, but Daddy developed a brain tumor and had to cut back on how many hours he could work. It took several years for him to fully recover. These were the years where I learned to just suck it up when things didn't go my way. Thinking back to that time I can't recall ever wanting to give up. My angel was working hard.

I believe the longest walk I ever had to make back then was from Vilano Beach to the post office on St. George Street to open P.O. Box 1407 and see if Daddy's check was in the box. When the check was there, the walk back to Vilano Beach was short. When the check didn't arrive, I thought I would never make it back to the cabin. These were some hard times, but there were more good times that almost totally blocked out the bad ones.

Crabbing and Fishing From P.J.'s Dock

Richard and I loved to fish off the dock. We didn't have rods and reels; we used hand lines to catch fish and crabs. I didn't own my first rod and reel until 1965 when I went to work for Southeastern Fisheries Association. P.J. Sr., who most people called "Blossom," saved us chicken necks and odd bones left over from the butcher shop he had in the back of his grocery store. Richard and I called him Mr. Manucy, not "Blossom," or our butts would have been tanned by Mama.

When we had crab bait, we scurried to the end of the dock unless I was working and couldn't get time off. But usually I found the time to help catch those delicious, large male blue-crabs. Mama was awesome at catching them. She always tied a chicken neck or bone to the line, putting it in the water near the bottom for a few minutes until she felt something move it around a little bit. Her touch was honed so that she could feel the slightest movement on the line.

She would slowly bring the white cotton line up until she saw the hungry blue-crab hanging on the chicken neck with his claws locked into the meat. Then, she eased the long wooden-handled crab net into the water just below and behind the crab and quickly shifted the net upward, bringing the crab to the surface and one step closer to a hot pot of water—all with one swift move. She deftly dumped the live, claw-snapping crab into a five-gallon bucket, slapping the lid back on so that the crab couldn't crawl out on the dock and try to take a bite out of our butts. It seemed she could put a crab in the bucket and lower her line for the next crab at the same time. She was that good.

Mama said, "The secret is gently moving the net in

back of the crab because his eyes are in the front, and he's more interested in the food than he should be." This operation would be repeated until there were 20-25 crabs in the bucket. Then, we would happily take the crazy-acting crabs back to the cabin.

Mama heated water in the one big pot she had and used tongs to place the live crabs in the pot. The crabs tried to climb out, but we poked them back in with the tongs or a spoon. They were fully cooked in a matter of minutes. Mama used some kind of homemade seasoning that made the whole cabin smell good. There were no picnic tables and no patio outside, so all the picking and eating was done inside the cabin at the little kitchen table. I remember we used lots of newspaper to catch all the drippings and crab smelling water. No matter how careful we were, and even though we had linoleum on the floor, the smell lingered for a good two days.

Picking fresh North River crabs is a real treat, and we ate everything we caught. We learned early on that "if you kill it, get ready to eat it." Mama made crab cakes using back fin and lump meat, but we ate all the dark claw meat as fast as we could crack the shell. I would bite down on the exposed meat of the claw until my teeth felt the cartilage. Then I'd pull the claw from my mouth, reaching for another one as quickly as possible before Richard got it. Sometimes, we put two claws in our mouths to get more meat. When we finished every last one, we put the crab shells back in the five-gallon bucket; walked to the end of the dock, and dumped them in the river. We watched catfish and other kinds of fish go crazy, fighting to get a fresh snack before the shells even hit the bottom. Blue crabs in the North River were plentiful. Most locals used the historically proven hand-line method to catch a mess of crabs for their families. Catching crabs today in the same way and same place is a wonderful part of life.

Every now and then, at the last of the rising tide or first of the falling tide, when most of the marsh grass was underwater, we put a bobber, small hook, split shot, and piece of shrimp on a hand line. We caught two-pound flounders and speckled trout that were working near the oyster bars. This was always fun because we felt every pull of the fish on the thin cotton line that we held tightly with our young hands. We liked catching flounder, trout, and redfish. But more than catching them, we knew that after cleaning them, they would be in Mama's big black, crusty, lard-laden frying pan, turning crisp and golden on the outside with sweet, juicy white meat under the skin. Fresh, fried North River fish are so succulent that they melt in your mouth. For anyone who has never enjoyed this special fresh Vilano Beach seafood treat, I offer my condolences.

P.J. gave me bait shrimp practically for free, especially shrimp that died in the live bait well. I often took these small river shrimp back to Mama instead of fishing with them so that she could fry them for us. They had a hint of marsh grass, mixed with the aroma of a northeast wind, plus a special flavor only found in St. Augustine white river shrimp. When fishing or crabbing was available, we ate very well. When fresh fish were unavailable, we ate lots of Spam, potted meat, canned greens, macaroni and cheese, bags of potatoes from Hastings, and hoecake (the dish I liked best).

I always felt that hoecake was the best thing in the world, and I have missed eating it for the past few decades. Hoecake might have originated from an authentic Native American recipe using maize. Some have written that it got the name hoecake because in tough times it was cooked on the blade of a hoe. From what I have learned, the basic hoecake is made of cornmeal, water, and bacon fat. It becomes Johnnycake when you use eggs, sugar, and butter in the batter. I have not seen hoecake on the Food Network yet. Maybe a famous chef will make it sometime.

We occasionally got money for real food from my dear Aunt Pat Shugart. When that happened, Mama fried chicken in her special way. What a treat it was! I would dearly love to see Mama again standing at her small gas stove frying chicken as she did at the cabin on Vilano Beach. There was never a single piece of chicken left on the plate if Richard and I were present.

One thing I learned at an early age was to get to Mama's fried gizzards and second joint right away because it would be on the plate one minute and then gone. If Richard got to it first, it would be nothing but a sad memory. That did not happen very often.

Some things don't change over time. Recently, in the *Tallahassee Democrat* newspaper was a "Hagar the Horrible" cartoon. It showed Hagar and his son sitting on a rock on top of a mountain. The son said, "Dad, what does 'good timing' mean?" Hagar pointed his finger upward and said, "Good timing is being able to grab the last piece of chicken off the plate while pointing to an imaginary fly on the ceiling." Hagar is my man!

Shrimping with "Conch" Edge, a Master River Fisherman

P.J. Manucy needed live shrimp available for sport fishermen in order to maintain a steady flow of cash-paying customers. So, he told me I was going live bait shrimping with Conch Edge and would handle the oars. I was quite adept at rowing either sitting down or standing up in any direction at a fairly fast speed. I was 14, strong, and did whatever Conch Edge told me to do. He knew all of the creeks of North River better than anyone. After shrimping with him for a while, I thought he must be able to smell shrimp under the water because he always caught enough live shrimp to fill the fully aerated bait tanks on the dock.

Conch Edge was the kind of a man you rarely meet

more than once in a lifetime. He was special to me because he knew everything about the river and fishing. He wasn't a big man, but he was tough and quiet. I don't recall ever having an extended conversation with him, although I rowed and poled the shrimp barge with him up and down many, many creeks over several years. I only remember a few words he spoke which had to do with the way I was positioning the boat. He would say "easy" or "stop" or "go." I knew what he meant and must have done it well because he always wanted me to go with him instead of anyone else. He never told me I did a good job, but in those days, you were expected to do a good job. When you are young, you sometimes think you are appreciated only if someone tells you so, but when you mature, it's easier to read body language or even a look that says, "Good job."

Riverside Fish Camp's slow-moving shrimp barge was about sixteen feet long, five feet wide in the middle, and tapered at the bow. It had a large live well in the center to keep the shrimp after they were caught in Conch's cast net and quickly and carefully shucked into the well. The bottom of the live bait compartment was full of holes so that water could constantly flow in and out. There was a flat plywood platform in the bow where Conch stood to cast his 12-foot net. I thought he was an old man at the time, but he could stand and throw the net for hours, stopping only if we motored to another creek after the tide or wind changed.

In the stern portion of the boat, there was a set of oar locks, two seven-foot oars, and a wooden seat if I wanted to sit down and row with the bow at my back. Most of the time, I rowed standing up and looked forward so I could see where Conch wanted me to position the boat. If he had the lead line in his teeth, he would nod his head to tell me how near to ease up to the shore.

I remember shrimping far up Robinson and Casacola Creeks and in the mouth of Oscar Masters, Willis, Medici, and Carcaba creeks. They are all north of Riverside Fish Camp on the east side of the river. While writing this account, I remembered the names of Robinson and Casacola Creeks, but had to call two high school and brick-laying buddies, Sonny Burchfield and Barry Masters, to help me recall the names of the other creeks.

For the trip to and from the faraway creeks, we used a ten-horsepower Evinrude outboard motor that hummed like a race car. However, the barge moved at a slow speed so that the water in the well didn't rush out and kill the shrimp. The old Evinrude took us miles up North River and all the way around St. Augustine's bayfront into the San Sebastian River, ending up at the Mill Creek Bridge on State Road 16 where shrimping was often fantastic.

An Unforgettable Shrimping Experience

One Saturday morning, P.J. said, "Take the live shrimp barge from Riverside Fish Camp to the State Road sixteen Bridge over the San Sebastian River. Then, wait until after lunch when the tide is right." The cold front that passed through the day before created an abundance of shrimp congregated by the thousands in the deep holes in certain oyster beds.

I cranked the faithful Evinrude with a few hard pulls and then untied the boat. After slipping under the Vilano Beach Bridge, I skillfully navigated the narrow channel on the west bank of the Matanzas River that runs very close to the ancient and massive coquina stone walls of the fort. After clearing the Bridge of Lions, I followed the inside channel until I saw Flagler Hospital. Then, I steered eastward into the Intercoastal Waterway that took me to the mouth of the always flowing, dark waters of the San Sebastian River.

The San Sebastian had many curves and bends, but there was plenty of water even at low tide. I usually saw offshore shrimp trawlers and snapper boats moored at Salvador's Seafood next to the King Street Bridge. Master boat-builder, Harry Xynides, usually had a boat under construction at his yard. It took about two hours to take the shrimp barge from Vilano Beach to State Road 16, where P.J. and Conch Edge waited for me on the bridge.

As soon as they saw me idling toward them, Conch walked down to the water's edge and jumped into the boat like a cat jumping off a fence. He grabbed his net while I raised the motor up on the transom. I then grabbed my oars without anyone saying a word. P.J. waited for us to fill up the live bait well with shrimp. Afterward, he and Conch would drive back to Vilano Beach in his Model A dune buggy while I brought the boat back to Riverside Fish Camp. I was apprehensive about the night trip through narrow channels but said nothing about my fears. Suck it up and move on.

As soon as Conch got settled in the boat, the wind picked up, making it impossible to hold the big shrimp barge in one spot with my oars. Conch said, "Get overboard and hold the boat in place while I cast the net." The water was cold and up to my shoulders, so it was all I could do to hold the heavy barge steady.

For some reason, maybe providence, after Conch had made about ten casts, I looked in back of me and saw a large alligator with big black eyes fifty feet from where I was standing in the water holding the boat. The alligator was motionless, but when I saw its widely separated eyes, the top of its ugly bumpy head, and its armored body, I jumped in the boat before you could count to one. It's amazing how much strength you have when you are terrified. After I pulled my cold, drenching wet body to a full standing position, I looked over on the bridge and saw P.J. chuckling. I glared at him as hard as a teenage river rat could glare at his boss. He did not even ask if I was going to get back in the water because he read my body language and knew there was no way, unless someone threw me in, and at that moment it would have taken several full grown folks to get me back in the water.

P.J. said, "I had my eye on it and would have told you to jump in the boat if he started to move any closer." I didn't say anything to P.J., but I didn't get back in the water then, or ever again, at that place. I'm not sure if Conch ever saw the gator because he was casting his net in the opposite direction. I could have been gator bait. Then what would all of my children and grandchildren and great-grandchildren have done?

I had another scare as I brought the live shrimp barge back from the San Sebastian River that night. I didn't use running lights because we didn't have any on the boat, and if we would have, their reflection would have made it harder for me to see. The lights on shore caused enough problems because the inside channel next to the fort was narrow in several places, particularly at low tide.

I was turning the throttle to the wide open position, trying to get the boat on a plane in the shallow water, when all of a sudden, something big and white flew up out of the pitch black night and landed in the boat flopping all over the floor, on my feet, and up against the sides of the boat. I lifted my feet and cut the throttle to idle speed in case one of us had to get some relief by going overboard. Did I mention there were never any life preservers on board?

My heart was pounding so loud I could hear it. I almost jumped out of the boat until I realized a full-grown flounder had been spooked and jumped straight up near the bow, falling into the stern of the boat where I happened to be sitting. I popped the big fish a couple of times with the oar. It calmed down immediately. Of course, I was delighted to clean the fish later that night and put it on ice at P.J.'s until I retrieved it the next morning. That big, thick white-meat flounder was delicious when Mama fried it the next night for our supper.

Catching Fiddler Crabs

The massive mud flat south of the Riverside Fish Camp dock was home to at least 100,000 fiddler crabs at low tide. Fiddler crabs are excellent bait for sheepshead but a devil to catch by hand if the mud is soft and deep. They quickly crawl into their mud holes when humans come near. Sometimes, the hole is too deep to dig the fiddler out with your finger. They remind me a little bit of soldiers scrambling for a foxhole when they hear incoming mortar rounds.

Finger-digging for fiddler crabs was a sure way to get a few claw bites, but it didn't hurt nearly as much as a bite from a blue crab or, worst of all, a stone crab. We didn't see too many stone crabs, but we knew their powerful claw could take a teenager's finger off. We were told as kids that if a stone crab bites you, it won't let go until the sun goes down. Of course, we were told a lot of things as kids just to keep us in line.

The shallow water in front of the mud flats had

outcroppings of live oysters among a profusion of dead oyster shells poised to cut your feet if you stepped on them when chasing down fiddlers. We always had a variety of cuts on our arms, hands, and legs, so it's a wonder we didn't develop some dreaded disease. Lucky for us the water back then was less polluted than today.

P.J. paid out a little bit of money for catching fiddlers, maybe enough for a Moon Pie and an RC Cola, but we enjoyed getting muddy and stinky as much as getting the money. We were being paid for having fun. How can anyone beat that?

Mystical Sea Cows

We didn't swim in the river during the "sea cow" migration up and down the North River. The big, cumbersome, beautiful manatees swam next to the dock at least two times a year. When they arrived and the word got out, everyone rambled out to the end of the dock to watch them cavort and eat the lettuce offerings by the locals. As big as they were, they were totally graceful. It was like watching a dancer. We didn't know much about these special critters, except we could see that they were big, so we gave them plenty of room. We knew they didn't have big pointed teeth like sharks and we never heard of them hurting anyone, but they were so big that we didn't dare bother them. Nobody we knew ever harmed one of these creatures, and I certainly never heard of anyone killing one of them. All of us who worked around the water were taught early on not to kill any critter that we didn't intend to eat. Killing a critter for fun is dumb.

The river was theirs for as long as they stayed around. I don't recall anyone playing or swimming with the manatees back in those days like they do now in Crystal River, Florida. I do remember floating lettuce on the water to get them to come to the surface so that we could see their whiskered faces and humongous bodies. Their eyes penetrated mine, and I wondered how anything so big could be so gentle. Manatees have always been a special animal to me because I bonded with them many, many years ago at Riverside Fish Camp on Vilano Beach.

P.J. Manucy, a Real Hero

On numerous occasions, Mama told my baby sister, Lessie, in the strongest possible words to never go out on the dock without a grownup, which included me or Richard. As happens so often with kids, Lessie thought she was big enough to go out on the dock and she fell into the dark river. I didn't see her fall in because I was cleaning up stuff in the motor storage room. But my eye did catch P.J. Manucy, Jr. sprinting toward the dock from his house like an Olympic runner, trying to get the watch off his wrist. He couldn't get the watch off. I stopped what I was doing and followed him out to the end of the dock as fast as I could run. I knew something was wrong. Then

I saw him dive into the water and come up with a very wet, very scared, very lucky, and very sweet Lesta Ann Jones in his arms. She would have drowned if not for P.J. Manucy. God held her in the palms of His hands that day through the strong arms of P.J. Manucy. It was a miracle.

In less than one minute, P.J.'s quick, brave action saved my sister Lessie's life. He was my hero forever after that, and always will be. He ruined his watch because not much was waterproof in those days. I hoped to someday earn enough money to buy him a new watch, but he died before I was able to do so.

P.J. performed a courageous act that affected many lives. I pray that he and his wonderful wife, Sadie, are at peace and their souls, through the mercy of God, rest in peace.

Leaving Vilano Beach

I met a lot of neat guys in 1949 who convinced me to go back to high school after I was expelled from Ketterlinus High. They asked me to give St. Joseph's Academy a try. Joe Kehoe, Paul Justice, and Paul Noble opened up a new world for me and helped me meet new people. During that summer, I met five girls from St. Joseph's Academy who came to Vilano Beach to swim and get a tan. This is when I met Malinda Louise Usina, who has been my wife since May 28, 1955. That day remains the happiest of my life.

LIVING AT THE FOOT OF THE BRIDGE

Mama, Richard, Lessie, and I moved to North St. Augustine (North City) in 1950. We unpacked our meager goods into a very old and modest five-room house in back of P.J. Manucy Sr's grocery store on San Marco Avenue. The screened porch had a table and three big rocking chairs. From the front porch you could see Russell's Bar B Que, the home of the best hamburgers in the world. We felt like we had moved into the Taj Mahal. The icing on the cake was the short walk to town and Davis Shores, which meant no more hitchhiking late at night from downtown to Vilano Beach.

Even though our cabin on Vilano Beach was small, the water was sulphurous, and money was scarce, some of my fondest memories happened when I lived at the foot of the bridge.

Our home on Vilano Beach, Florida

A Taste of Shrimp That Lasts a Lifetime

SUMMERTIME MEANT LARGE, succulent white shrimp in a bed of ice at Salvador's Seafood Market on West King Street and at Riverside Fish Camp on Vilano Beach if you happened to be around when P.J Manucy's F/V Hoonya unloaded the day's catch.

I was fourteen years old, living at the foot of the Vilano Beach Bridge in one of the white wooden cabins behind P.J. Sr's. store on the north side of Highway AIA. If Mama went to town with Sadie Manucy on Friday afternoon she always stopped by Salvador's to buy fresh white shrimp. Seemed like we always had fish on Friday and I wasn't even a Catholic back then.

Mama was usually greeted by Felix Salvador who had funny things to say or worldly advice to offer if he wasn't hollering at one of the helpers to bring more ice to put on top of the fish and shrimp. He weighed the shrimp on a rusty scale then dumped them on a foot-high stack of newspapers and quickly rolled them up in four or five pages to keep them cold. The old newspapers were called the "mullet wrappers" but in our case it was a shrimp wrapper.

When Mama returned from town, Richard, my younger brother and I, stood at the old, chipped porcelain sink and helped her peel the big shrimp. We usually stuck our finger with the sharp horn on the head of the shrimp a time or two during the process. We were used to getting pricked but the end product was worth a little drop of blood or two. Baby sister, Lessie, was too young to peel shrimp so she and her best bud, Linda Manucy, played dress-up with ladies clothes, hats and high heel shoes that belonged to Sadie, Linda's mother.

Mama deveined the shrimp with a small knife, then cut them precisely to a certain depth on top of each shrimp so they would all curl up the same way and be fully cooked in just a few minutes. She used white lard to fry the shrimp in her one and only cast iron frying pan. All she added to the cracker meal was salt and pepper before she coated each shrimp. Mama had a way of holding the tail tight so that when she put the lightly dusted shrimp on a piece of wax paper the tail was always clean and easy to pick up from the platter after they were fried. We did not take a shrimp from the big platter until Mama sat down. Then it was time to taste the goodness on the table.

MINORCAN GUMBO FOR THE SOUL

There's something special about St. Augustine's white shrimp. The translucent shell is beautifully colored. The contrast of the dark eyes and reddish legs is prominent as you peel them. St. Augustine shrimp smell good when they are raw. When they are fresh they are slightly sweet, and not the least pungent. It must be the clean ocean water and what they ate during their brief twelve months of life that give them their superb taste.

As good as the raw shrimp smelled, I have no words adequate to describe the heavenly odor of fresh shrimp frying in first lard…in a small room…in a small cabin… on Vilano Beach. I loved watching the shrimp pile up in the big plate Mama kept next to the frying pan. If Richard or I reached for a shrimp before Mama put them on the table we either got a stern look or a tap on the hand with hot tongs. We were quick learners. It took me two years before I was smooth enough to hug her with one arm, slip a hot shrimp in my pants pocket with my free hand then walk outside to eat it. I felt she smiled, knowing exactly what I was doing but did not say a word. That's what Mamas do.

When I visit St. Augustine and eat Lonnie Pomar's shrimp at Osteen's, it is very close to the flavor and aroma I fondly remember. I'm sure there are a few other places you can get genuine St. Augustine shrimp for a while longer, but when all the shrimp boats are gone so will the opportunity to enjoy a seafood experience that's been available since St. Augustine offshore shrimping began in about 1922.

Salvador's Seafood Market is gone. Riverside Fish Camp, as I knew it, is gone. The opportunity for me to eat shrimp in such a nostalgic setting as the little cabin is gone, but not forgotten. I would give anything to stand by that old gas stove in P.J.'s cabin watching and listening to Mama's iron skillet fry shrimp. Actually, there is nothing I wouldn't give just to stand by my Mama again.

Me and Gary Cooper

IT WAS IN the spring of 1951 when the *St. Augustine Record* and radio station WFOY announced that *Distant Drums*, an epic movie about the Seminole Indian War, would be partially filmed on location in St. Augustine, Florida. I was 17 years old and in my junior year in high school.

The script required Captain Quincy Wyatt, played by Gary Cooper, and a small band of soldiers to blow up St. Augustine's Castillo de San Marcos and rescue the white prisoners held by the Seminoles. A hundred or so local citizens would be selected from a long line of applicants to become Gary Cooper's soldiers.

The director announced a casting call to select men who were able to scale the high coquina block walls of Castillo de San Marcos using only a knotted rope. The men selected as soldiers received union wages of approximately $35 per day. In 1951, the minimum wage in St. Augustine was probably about 75 cents an hour, so hundreds of men from the area arrived for the casting call. I wanted to be one of Gary Cooper's soldiers more than anything else in the world.

I was a strong, young athlete who had participated in all sports in high school. I had the strength to climb up the pockmarked coquina block fort wall that seemed fifty feet high. I had never tried anything like that before, but I really wanted to be selected so I could earn big money to buy pretty things for Malinda and something special for Momma, Richard and my sister, who was seven years old at the time.

The St. Joseph's Academy boys who wanted to try out for a part in the movie were excused from classes by Sister Mary Martha, the magnificent principal who helped turn many young people – including me – toward God and studies. All of the football players that got excused showed up bright and early at Castillo de San Marcos, which is a real fort never captured by the enemy, although the city of St. Augustine was sacked several times by pirates and the British.

We blended into the crowd of people milling around, waiting for the first call to line up to be selected or go home. I was wearing a Green Bay Packers baseball cap because I liked their green and gold colors, which were the same as my high school. The other football players were also wearing caps, primarily because we had decided to peroxide our hair for spring football practice. The other guys turned blond, but my hair was an ugly orange.

As the director approached, he told me to take off my cap. I did. He rolled his eyes toward the sky. He started walking on down the line and with a disgusted tone of voice, told me I could go home. I was absolutely devastated. One of the other guys whose hair was a normal blonde color was selected, but most of the others with dyed hair were cut.

I went home and asked Momma to help me dye my hair back to black. She had some kind of old hair dye, and after going through the process two or three times, the orange color vanished, never to return again.

The next day, I sprinted to the fort wearing different clothes and no baseball cap. I found a spot in the middle part of the long line, and when the director came to me, he asked if I had been there the day before. I said "No" because I was actually standing at a different place, so I really hadn't been "there" where he asked. He looked at me for a long minute and said, "Go get a uniform." Yes, I did fib a little bit, but I wanted and needed that job and money. And I *was* standing in a different spot from the previous day.

I hustled over to the wardrobe area, gave my name, address, and Social Security number, and was fitted for a soldier's uniform. They had a safe place for us to stash our street clothes. I was glad of that because I only owned one decent pair of khaki pants.

Talk about a very happy camper. I had to pinch myself to make sure I wasn't dreaming when I got to stand so close to Gary Cooper, Raoul Walsh, the famous director with a black patch over one eye, Richard Webb, Mari Aldon, and Arthur Hunnicutt, Jr. As long as they weren't shooting a scene, we could stand right next to any of them and take pictures.

I had an old Kodak box camera that Momma let me use. I stared at Gary Cooper. I had seen him in the theater as Sergeant York a decade earlier. He was my hero long before I ever imagined in my wildest dreams that I would be standing next to him in real life, being a bit player in his movie and that he would look at me and smile.

He was tall, lean, and moved like a man who knew what he was doing and where he was going. He was slightly balding with wavy hair and did not wear a wig. I didn't notice much makeup, and I was close enough to see his blue eyes. His face crinkled when he smiled at Mari Aldon.

He smiled a lot, and I never heard him say a cross word, nor did I hear any loud or obscene language by the director or from any of the people handling the lights and camera equipment.

I took a picture of Gary Cooper talking to Mari Aldon about a scene they were shooting. I stood there, quiet as a spider, listening to them talk about their work. My absolute enthusiasm kept my hands steady when the shutter

◄ MINORCAN GUMBO FOR THE SOUL

clicked. Thankfully, the picture didn't come out blurry. There was no such thing as a telephoto lens for a Kodak box camera, which meant that I was very close when I had that once-in-a-lifetime experience.

Gary Cooper's hat rests on the chair in the photo. The man wearing a white shirt with his back to me snapping the picture was the person who selected me to be in the movie on my second try.

Photo by Bobby Jones, 1951.

ME AND GARY COOPER

Richard Webb was cast as Richard Tufts, a US Naval Officer assigned to lead Gary Cooper to a rescue boat in Lake Okeechobee. Webb was friendly and seemed to enjoy talking to many of us. He played "Captain Midnight" on TV in the early 1950s and starred in many other movies before he took his own life in 1993.

Lt. Richard Tufts (Richard Webb) and Bobby Jones the Indian fighter

I was part of the "supporting cast." In the trailer, I found on Google.com that I am one of the men (boys) running across the bridge at the Castillo de San Marcos in St. Augustine, but you wouldn't know it unless I told you. The scene lasts a second or two, but we must have done ten takes before Director Walsh was satisfied.

At the end of the day's shooting, I turned in my

uniform, slipped on my khaki pants and white tee shirt, and ran the five or six blocks home to Osceola Street. It came to me as I was writing this paragraph that the Holy Spirit has a sense of humor because I was guided to be in a movie about the Seminole Indians while I lived on Osceola Street. It is uncanny that I never realized that coincidence before.

I officially met Gary Cooper at Malinda Usina's house on Davis Shores after the second day of shooting. Malinda and I had been sweethearts for over a year, so she invited me to the party her parents hosted for Cooper and his entourage. Malinda and I were totally thrilled to be in the same room with Gary Cooper at her home on Matanzas Bay. We stood discreetly in the background, watching and listening to everything. We were so excited it's impossible to describe our feelings.

I vividly remember how handsome and vibrant Cooper was. He wore light-colored trousers, an open-collared shirt, and a blue jacket with gold buttons. He sat on one of the bar stools in the kitchen, surrounded by the other stars in the movie, telling stories and holding court for everyone in the big, open Florida room.

We were mesmerized as we moved close enough to where he sat to eavesdrop. People told jokes and laughed loudly. The constant banter between the Hollywood visitors and Charlie Usina's guests was just like a movie to me ... except I was somehow in the scene, although very much on the periphery. Everyone was laughing, drinking whiskey, and completely enjoying the moment. I cannot remember all the people who were there, but I'm sure Carver Harris, Bob Eastman, Norton Baskin, W.I. Drysdale, Tony Meitin, L.C. Ringhaver, Bob Curtan, Put Calhoun, and so many other St. Augustine movers and shakers who were friends of Charlie and Phyllis Usina.

After a couple of hours, Malinda and I went outside and walked along the sea wall, holding hands and enjoying the evening more than anyone. We were in love, and we were together on a starlit evening looking at the St. Augustine skyline that we both loved. It was an exceptional evening and a special "Me and Gary Cooper" experience.

An Evening to Remember

IN THE SPRING of 1951, I had been going steady with Malinda for over a year. There are many, many happy moments in our longstanding love affair that are super sweet, but there are certain moments branded into the strongest cells of my brain that are above and beyond sweet. This short story is about one of those special moments.

St. Augustine's Ponce de Leon Golf Course was famous since it was built in 1916. It was designed by Donald Ross, one of the best designers of that era. Before it became a golf course, it was a Native American village known as Capuaca, followed by a plantation of the same name. Of course, I didn't know that in 1951.

The first time I stepped on that historical land was when I tried to be a caddy at the Ponce course in 1949, but the huge alligator leather bag full of clubs, balls, and God-knows-what-all was too heavy for me to carry and walk eighteen holes twice a day. I remember the $3 tip was the hardest money I had ever made.

AN EVENING TO REMEMBER

I didn't know anything about the rules of golf, so my one and only caddy experience must have been laughable. Besides, the regular caddies didn't appreciate me trying to take their jobs.

The next time I returned to the Ponce de Leon clubhouse was when Papa and Mimi Usina invited me to go with them as Mindy's escort to the regular Saturday night dinner party at the club house. I was so excited that I didn't know what to do. I was not all that sure about the proper etiquette, but I did have a sense for good manners, which I learned from my mother. I didn't know which utensil to use first, but Mindy whispered, "Follow my lead if you have any doubts." That might have been when I learned to start at the outside line of forks or spoons and work inward.

I did have a blue sport coat and tie, and I shined my well-worn black shoes and walked from my house on San Marco Avenue in North City to Mindy's house across the Bridge of Lions on Davis Shores. It was a hop, skip, and a jump after the years I walked from Vilano Beach to Davis Shores to visit Miss Mindy, hoping to get a kiss and a squeeze if nobody was looking.

Mr. Usina asked me to drive the car. I was thrilled driving north on US 1. About two miles past State Road 16 going north, I turned into the palm tree-lined shell road surrounded by shrubs and well-kept golf greens on both sides. The Ponce de Leon clubhouse was located at the end of the road not too far from the water's edge.

I remember parking next to a large white clapboard building with lots of fully opened windows. The night sea breeze came gently off the marsh grass near the water's edge keeping everyone cool. We walked past the massive glass doors, into a room of beautiful fresh, floral arrangements. The Drysdales and Curtans were with us, plus two other couples at the table.

I stayed close to Mindy, which is something I have done and enjoyed since she was fifteen. We drank Cokes, while the adults drank all kinds of strange cocktails. We were served a variety of scrumptious appetizers, including a shrimp cocktail with the biggest shrimp I had ever seen. The main entrée was tender, rare, prime roast beef, which was a first for me. Finally, we enjoyed the desserts that were created by renowned pastry chefs at the world-class Ponce de Leon Hotel's kitchen downtown.

There was a live band–probably Tony Nobile's orchestra. Tony's orchestra was very popular and played for all of the Ponce de Leon functions. Mindy and I danced nearly every dance because that's what we did every Friday night at SJA's Teen Town. Besides, it was acceptable to hold her in my arms in public as long as we were dancing. We knew all of the dances and did the jitterbug as well as anybody else in town. We truly fit together. I could twirl her around with my left or right hand and slip her under my arm to the beat of the music. We had a ball!

AN EVENING TO REMEMBER

I was Cinderfella and knew I would return to normal at the end of the evening. That was okay and a small price to pay for an evening to remember for a lifetime.

Later, after all of the food had been consumed, the tables were cleared, and the adults were drinking after dinner cocktails or coffee, Maestro Tony Nobile announced a jitterbug contest. Of course, everyone at our table insisted that Mindy and I participate. What an absolute thrill! It was hard for me to imagine that here I was with the girl I loved at a party of St. Augustine leaders. I didn't have five cents in my pocket, but no money was needed. I still cannot find the perfect words to explain how wonderful I felt that entire evening.

The music began. The men and women made their way to the dance floor. We were the youngest couple. The orchestra was at one end of the long, bright room, and tables full of people turned their chairs around to face us.

I don't remember the name of the song, but it was a fast one. We went into our practiced routine. We had about five or six different moves. It was just a matter of doing them correctly, changing the sequence every now and then and letting our happy feet do the talking.

And do the talking they did! The song was very long. We were both breathing hard and sweating profusely when the contest ended.

Five minutes after the music stopped the judges cast

their votes. They announced the unanimous winners: "Malinda Usina and Bobby Jones." Everyone at our table stood and applauded. I didn't shed a tear that I remember, but I have shed one or two over the years just thinking about that special evening. It was one beautiful moment in our journey through life together.

A God Thing in Philadelphia

I WAS IN Cherry Point, North Carolina USMC base for two weeks of summer training in the USMC Reserve. I was 17 and a junior at St. Joseph's Academy in St. Augustine, Florida.

As a member of VMF Squadron 144, I was stationed at Jacksonville, Florida. My squadron was composed of F-4U Corsairs. I was being taught maintenance of this famous WW II fighter aircraft, but not allowed to work unless it was under the direct supervision of the sergeant in charge.

PFC Jimmy Sills, who lived in Green Cove Springs, was a good friend. He had a sister who lived in Hartford, Connecticut and asked me if I would like to hitchhike to Hartford to spend the weekend. We could leave the base at 1630 hours (4:30 p.m. for you civilians) on Friday and be back for muster at 0700 hours on Monday. I had never been north of where I was in Cherry Point so I said, "Sure." I did not realize it was over 600 miles away.

◀ MINORCAN GUMBO FOR THE SOUL

We wore our uniform and carried a small bag with a change of socks and underwear, comb, toothbrush and some smell-good, probably Old Spice. We had no trouble hitching a ride the moment we stepped off the base and stuck out our thumbs. As I recall, everybody who gave us a ride was nice. One man even bought us a meal at a gas station. I think we got to Jimmy's sister's house around breakfast time on Saturday. We spent the day with her family and enjoyed several great meals which were appreciated after eating all our meals the past week at the mess hall.

We left a few hours after supper to avoid being AWOL. We preferred to return early. It wasn't as easy hitching a ride at night and it was thirty minutes or so before a 18- wheeler truck driver stopped and picked us up. He was headed to Philadelphia and said he would be glad to take us that far. We were grateful. And tired.

It was around midnight when he reached his destination. We climbed out of the big truck and walked to the streetlight and started hitching for a ride again. Neither of us had been to Philadelphia before. We had no idea where we were. We knew we had to go south so we kept our thumbs out with big smiles on our faces hoping and praying for a ride.

It wasn't long before a big car stopped. The passenger in the back seat asked us where we were headed. I said Cherry Point, North Carolina. He said 'get in' so we opened the door to the back seat. He was a very big black

A GOD THING IN PHILADELPHIA

man. Jimmy and I looked at each other, shrugged our shoulders and got in. It did not dawn on me that anything could go wrong in a big northern city, with a car full of black men, driving us to someplace of which we had no idea. We hoped we were headed south.

I sat next to the big man in the back. He asked where we were from and what we were doing in that part of town. I told him I was from St. Augustine and Jimmy was from Green Cove Springs. We had visited Jimmy's sister in Hartford and the truck driver who gave us our first lift dropped us off where we were picked up. He chuckled and said it was nice to meet a couple of southern boys. We talked for what seemed an hour about the Marines and how much we liked working on the Corsairs. After we reached a major intersection he stopped the car. He told us the name of the highway and said we should be all right now. He smiled and the car drove away.

At the time I didn't think too much about that encounter. Maybe that is all it was; just another Good Samaritan helping out a couple of strangers. But over the years that encounter keeps floating back. I believe those good men in that big car saw two young Marines in a place where they shouldn't be and decided to take them out of harm's way. If so, that's a God Thing. My heart tells me that is exactly what happened.

For the men who drove us through Philadelphia, whoever you were and wherever you are, God Bless.

Sonny Burchfield

CLARENCE EDWARD "SONNY" Burchfield has been my friend since 1951 when we played high school football at St. Joseph's Academy in St. Augustine, Florida. Way back then, Sonny lived in a two-story, white clapboard house on San Marco Avenue.

Since he is two years younger, we didn't run with the same crowd as pre-teens when I lived near him at 37 Sylvan Drive in the mid 1940s. Two years makes all the difference in the world when you are young.

Our lifelong friendship began on a hot, dirt football practice field adjoining the St. Joseph's Academy Lyceum on St. George Street. We learned basic football plays and some manly discipline from Coach Angelo Massaro, a New York native who came to St. Augustine after honorably serving in the USMC. He was ramrod straight and a great role model.

He was recommended to St. Joseph's Academy by Dr. Jim DeVito, one of the greatest MDs ever, to be the school's first full-time Civics teacher and coach of all athletics. Coach Massaro taught Civics with great feeling, serving the America that the USMC honed to a fine blade.

Today, Sonny Burchfield is blessed with a taut, muscular body, a full head of hair, and probably weighs the same as when he was twenty-one years old. He is a nifty dancer who still loves line dancing and can even teach it. He is generally a man of few words unless he is arguing with Barry Masters or Bucky Powers over some fine point pertaining to electronics or life ... or after he has had a few pulls on the old wine bottle. Both of us like a little fruit of the vine every now and then, but we never drink unless we are with someone ... or alone.

Sonny has a great mind for technical details and an overdose of common sense, allowing him to fix anything that can be fixed. He has had this skill since he was old enough to pick up a wrench and screwdriver. In high school, he had a black Model A Ford Coupe with the standard rumble seat that could hold two people if they didn't mind rubbing fannies. He worked constantly to keep it running with bailing wire and a quart of gas. Had duct tape been invented back then, the car might have been shiny gray and dull black. I can still hear the special sound that only a Model A makes when hitting on all four cylinders.

Sonny and I maintained our friendship after high school while I worked at McCarter's Sealtest Dairy before receiving my military orders and boarding a big

MINORCAN GUMBO FOR THE SOUL

Greyhound bus headed to Parris Island Training.

I arrived at the USMC training depot in September of 1953, weighing in at 235 pounds. I spent twelve weeks of intense training and graduated at 189 pounds. Two years later, after fighting the battle of US 1 and the rum battles of Guantanamo Bay, Cuba, while serving on the CVE USS Saipan, I was proud to receive an Honorable Discharge. While I was in the Corps, Sonny was completing his bricklayer/masonry apprenticeship and serving in the Florida National Guard.

During those times when I was able to catch a ride or hitchhike for a weekend from Opa Locka Air Base in Miami where I was stationed to St. Augustine to see Malinda, we went on double dates with Sonny. Many of the parties we attended later on brought us together with Sonny's future love, Phyllis Pacetti. Sonny has always been a "no problem" kind of a person, unless you get him mad, which isn't easy to do.

Our friendship strengthened when I began my masonry apprenticeship. In those first years, I worked with Sonny on the same job quite often. A few years later, Sonny and I were the main two masons for "Coot" Davis and worked on many different construction jobs together. We could lay block, brick, plaster, stucco, and finish cement, which is what I liked least of all. We poured more than 50 yards of concrete at the Florida School for the Deaf & Blind one day and didn't finish until 11:00 p.m.

Those were good years and good times, even though our aching muscles had a different story to tell.

From 1956 to 1957, Sonny was at our apartment on 22 Central Avenue almost every evening. On Monday nights, when he had his weekly drill with the Florida National Guard, he would come by at about 6:00 p.m. and watch "Gunsmoke" and "Have Gun Will Travel" on our black and white Zenith television set. Then, he would jump in his Ford and leave just in time to make muster. It was an unbroken ritual for over a year.

I would go out to his house on Tuesday nights to help him on a project or just shoot the bull and listen to music.

It was near Mindy's birthday in January 1956 when, in her sweetest, nicest voice and deeply concerned look from those big, beautiful brown eyes, she said, "Do you love Sonny more than you love me because he certainly sees you more than I do?" It wasn't long before I started spending more time at 22 Central Avenue and less in Sonny's workshop.

My changed lifestyle had many positive results and probably added to the number of children in the Jones household.

A true friendship like the one I have with Sonny is something that lasts even if you are apart for long periods of time. A bonded friendship has no bounds and no hard and fast rules or requirements.

Sonny and Phyllis were starting their own family

around 1960. Mindy and I already had Mike and Cindy, and Laurie was on the way. I think Laurie and Sonny's daughter, Kelly, are about the same age.

When I joined the St. Augustine Jaycees, Malinda and I started working and playing with another group of men and women who were joined at the hip through all of the Jaycee activities. Sonny had more to do and not enough time for Jaycees, so our relationship was simply put on hold for a few years, even though we got together at parties with Fred and Marianne Brinkhoff or with Bucky and Nancy Powers.

Many times, we went to Leonard and Connie Shugart's house for food and drinks and singing about Uncle Bud. We danced on their patio and laughed about the time Sonny and Leonard tried to brew beer and it exploded late one night in the closet. Besides being scared by the late night explosion, the smell and mess was a monumental cleanup project. Thereafter, I think the homemade brew-making paraphernalia was kept outside.

Those were good times, producing more laughs over a few years than some folks get in a lifetime. There are also special memories of many weekends spent skiing in Matanzas Bay and making a few trips up the St. Johns or Ocklawaha Rivers.

When the Jones family moved to Tulsa, Oklahoma in 1963 and then to Tallahassee in 1964, there wasn't much time for visits except each summer. We happily went back to St. Augustine to stay in the tiny Usina cottage behind the dune line on St. Augustine Beach on 14th Lane.

We got together often during the summer. One particular summer after we had spent the previous years crowded into the very small beach cottage, Sonny, Bucky Powers, Donald Germaine, and Fred Brinkhoff helped build a large family room that doubled the size of the house. It was a splendid addition, and I still drive by and look at it every time I get to St. Augustine. We had so many fun times in that big, wide-open, rectangular room.

The "Minorcan Construction Company," a not-for-profit, unorganized group of great guys, helped many a struggling couple live a better life through their generous gifts of time and know-how.

Through the years, though not often enough, we have been able to get together with Sonny and Phyllis and friends at Alligator Point for some great fishing and the usual cooking, plumbing, or electrical project, waiting for the Minorcan's visit.

Sonny and I, along with about six other friends, made a memorable ski trip to Steamboat Springs, Colorado and to Big Sky, Montana. Sonny is still an athlete and can traverse the toughest of slopes. Roger Newton from Apalachicola and Dale Bradbury from St. Augustine were in the group.

Two incidents stand out. The first was when Dale badly sprained his ankle. I had come down the same hill as he was on, but when he fell, I couldn't stop in time and get back up the slope to him. It was frustrating because I was just learning to ski and couldn't help. Several others had the same thing happen to them, but Fred was able to stop close enough to Dale and stayed with him until the ski patrol arrived. That was the end of skiing for Dale and the beginning of a difficult trip home.

The other incident occurred when Roger Newton thought he could ski with the big boys, so he followed Sonny to a Black Diamond slope. As Roger approached the edge of this particular treacherous run, he looked down at how steep it was. He didn't want to go down and asked Sonny, "What should I do?" Sonny glanced at the hill and looked at Roger. With a sly grin on his face, he slowly said to Roger, "Just do the best you can."

Roger came down mostly on his butt with his skis tucked securely under his arms. It was very, very steep. He stayed with us green slope guys from then on.

Sonny and I are now in our golden years. On many occasions, we have said that people have to be tough to get old. Aging is definitely not for sissies! We still try to get together at least once a year at Alligator Point for more grouper fishing, but we don't always make it. We have opportunities in North Carolina when our families get together for cards, mullet, or some other Minorcan feast. We are also able to ride to the top of Double Knob and other steep mountains on Honda 4 x 4 ATVs. What a rush!

SONNY BURCHFIELD

Sonny, Barry, Buddy Masters, and I (with great help from Gary Usina, Sr. and Fred Brinkhoff) built a large fireplace for Doug and Karen Smith at their house in Banner Elk, North Carolina. It was a very nostalgic experience being on the scaffold with high school classmates who are all such fine old men now. I worked with most of them in the masonry trade in my youth and relived a unique and wonderful opportunity to once again spread mud and lay bricks with the pros. This is another memory I shall cherish.

Sonny has a lot of friends. He is generous with his time, talent, and tools. His garage is full of saws, sanders, and routers that get a full workout not only from him, but from almost everyone in the neighborhood. I hope to get over there soon and spend a few days with this special friend who still has the same smile on his face he had when I met him over 69 years ago. God bless you, Sonny Burchfield.

Graduation Day USMC Training Depot, Parris Island, South Carolina

THE SOUTH CAROLINA sun was bright orange against a cloudless blue sky, but the wind off the salt marsh was frigid. The Marine Corps band marched behind the Colors. They wore dress blue uniforms and played highly polished musical instruments. Their rendition of "Under the Double Eagle March" gave me gooseflesh and a proud heart.

As the band approached our bleacher with brass horns blaring, I felt a few tears trickle down my chilly face. I really love marching music even when I'm not marching. Being in my graduation uniform with hundreds of other Marines on the historic Parade Ground at Parris Island was a moment in life that comes but once and only to the young.

GRADUATION DAY USMC TRAINING DEPOT, PARRIS ISLAND, SOUTH CAROLINA ➤

As my mind drifted into deep feelings about my country and my heritage, I wondered just how many young men had trained at Parris Island since it was established in 1891. I pondered if they felt the same spirit permeating the parade ground.

I had patriotic feelings so strong within me that breathing was difficult. In retrospect, this was a paradoxical moment for me as I had just finished being trained to kill in order to keep peace. These opposites were confronted, examined and balanced.

It was Platoon 423's Boot Camp graduation day on January 15th, 1954. That was over sixty-four years ago, but the smell of Cosmoline on the M-1 rifles, the heat of the tarmac on the parade grounds, and the pungent odor of marsh grass still lingers. There were sixty-eight young men graduating out of a class that started with seventy boys.

As I stood proud and at rigid attention on the top row in full dress greens with all of the other young Marines, I thought about the last twelve weeks on Parris Island. I easily recognized the improvement that those intense weeks of military training and discipline had made on my mind, my soul, and my body. I thought of how much I had learned in such a short period of time. To top it off, I learned that I was selected as the Outstanding Recruit for Platoon 423 by the drill instructors and our commanding officer. I was doubly proud to be who I was on that special

MINORCAN GUMBO FOR THE SOUL

day in 1954. It was one of the proudest moments of my life. Platoon 423 had made it through by working together for each other and the Corps.

My graduation was three days after Mindy's birthday and a brief twenty days after the first Christmas I ever spent away from home. It would be just a few hours before I boarded the train for Jacksonville, Florida, where Mindy and her parents would meet me and take me to St. Augustine. Momma was living on Osceola Street and working for the Florida National Guard. I was anxious to see her, Richard, and Lessie. This remains one of the proudest days of my life.

PFC R.P. Jones 1124182

GRADUATION DAY USMC TRAINING DEPOT, PARRIS ISLAND, SOUTH CAROLINA

Platoon 423—Jones top row far left.

Bobby, Mike, Glenn, and Saint Christopher

MINDY AND I left Tallahassee after work one Friday in 1968 with our five young children to spend the weekend at our St. Augustine Beach cottage. With the heavy traffic on Jacksonville's Beaver Street, it took four hours from Tallahassee to St. Augustine, which was the fastest way to get there until Interstate 10 was completed. We arrived at our cottage on 14th Lane around 9:30 p.m.

We drove to St. Augustine almost every weekend to visit family and friends, but mostly to be with Mimi, Mindy's mother, after Papa Usina died from cancer in 1966.

The cottage was a 30-year-old wooden frame house with yellow-shingle siding. This vintage pre-World War II house was built with roughhewn timbers that stood the test of time and decades of severe ocean weather. It rested a hundred feet west of the sand dunes. During high tides

BOBBY, MIKE, GLENN, AND SAINT CHRISTOPHER

from a northeaster, the angry ocean waves crashed over the dunes onto the small grass yard.

It had a large, uncovered front porch where we spent most of our time in the spring and summer, but it was too cold in the fall and winter to stay out very long except on those few sunny days when the wind blew from the west. When we were inside the 800-square foot cottage, our days were filled with card playing, cooking, laughter, and every conceivable activity imaginable by five beautiful, bright children blessed with extremely energetic parents.

On that bright, chilly Saturday morning, Mindy was happy to stay home with Cindy, Laurie, Mark, and Matt while Mike and I picked up Glenn Powers at his house near the St. Augustine Lighthouse for a day of fishing in the Matanzas River and an area known as Devil's Elbow. I hooked the 14-foot Billy Sanchez-built plywood boat to the company's 1961 Chevrolet Impala. We loaded our fishing equipment and food cooler in the boat and morphed into the roles of "hunters and gatherers."

Papa Usina bought this boat and the 18-horsepower Johnson outboard motor in the 1950s to use at his river cabin on the St. Johns River. After Papa died, the Jones family inherited Papa's boat. It was very special to me. I thought of him every time I looked at it and especially when I used it.

On that particular day, we planned to fish for puppy redfish near submerged oyster bars south of the San

◄ MINORCAN GUMBO FOR THE SOUL

Sebastian River. Then, we would work our way farther south past Devil's Elbow Fish Camp. Thank goodness, St. Christopher and Papa Usina were watching over us that Saturday.

I picked Glenn up at his house and talked to his parents, Bucky and Nancy Powers, for a few minutes. We pulled out of Bucky's driveway and drove across the road to the Anastasia Island Lighthouse Pier. We bought live and dead bait shrimp, cold drinks, sandwiches, Saltine crackers, Vienna Sausages, and lots of candy for the long voyage and hard day of fishing. I taught the kids early on that fishermen need plenty of sustenance, with fried chicken as the preferred food item. Alas, we didn't have any fried chicken that day.

I skillfully backed the car and boat trailer down the narrow concrete public ramp while Glenn stood on the narrow walkway holding the bow rope to keep the boat and all of our goods from drifting out into Salt Run.

As soon as I saw that Mike and Glenn had the boat secured alongside the slippery wooden walkway, I parked the car and brought them their coats, which they had left in the car after being told three times to bring warm clothes. Mike was twelve years old, and Glenn was about ten, so forgetting things was nothing new to them.

I pushed off from the ramp with an oar into deeper water. The dependable Johnson motor started with one pull. We were off to catch wary redfish, trout, and flounder. We

BOBBY, MIKE, GLENN, AND SAINT CHRISTOPHER

didn't have life preservers, but we had three green plastic floatable cushions to sit on and keep us safe. We had a set of seven-foot long, sturdy oars because it wasn't unusual for a mature outboard motor to become cantankerous every now and then. We needed a way to move away from the main channel and get to shore in the event of motor failure. We didn't have a radio, horn, whistle, or flares, and cell phones and GPS devices were not on the drawing board in 1968.

I told the boys to sit down facing me and pull their coats up to over their necks all the way to the back of their baseball caps. They didn't. They acted like those dogs you see on the road with their heads out of the automobile windows, yapping and snapping at the air.

We crossed the main channel near the inlet and headed west, staying close to the marsh grass until we were opposite the Castillo de San Marcos and beyond the sandbar on the east side of the small channel. I steered several hundred yards southeast to go under the main part of the Bridge of Lions. That way, my wake, as small as it was, didn't rock the boats tied up to the docks just south of the bridge or tied up at the marina. We were moving about fifteen miles an hour.

Mike picked up one of the oars and put it in the water in front of the bow of the boat, moving it back and forth in the water. I told him to put the oar down or it could throw him out of the boat. He didn't listen to my warning, and the next thing I knew, Michael Frederick Jones flew from the bow of the boat into the cold, deep water of Matanzas Bay. It happened in the blink of an eye.

To this day, I don't know how, but as soon as Mike hit the water behind the boat, I stood up on the wooden seat and did a back flip over the motor. I was in the water grabbing him as soon as he popped to the surface. His eyes were as wide as golf balls, and he furiously spit out salty river water and coughed. He was cold and scared, and the boat hauled butt down the river with a very surprised ten-year-old Glenn Powers sitting on the middle seat, probably wondering what in the hell had just happened.

Mike and I glanced at the boat and at each other. I held him next to me and knew instantly that we were in a bit of trouble with soaked winter coats and heavy work boots treading water in the shadow of the Bridge of Lions. I told him that I had him and that we would be fine.

Before panic descended on us and before I got my work boots off, Glenn jumped to the rear of the boat, slowed it down with the throttle; turned the boat expertly around, and headed straight toward us at a quick, but controlled speed. As soon as he got close, he threw two of the green seat cushions our way, which we thankfully grabbed. As it turned out, we didn't need them because Glenn had brought Papa's boat so close to us that we grabbed hold of the gunnels of that dry, wonderful boat.

Adrenaline is powerful. I must have generated a triple

BOBBY, MIKE, GLENN, AND SAINT CHRISTOPHER

dose because I easily grabbed Mike with my right hand and, without effort, picked him up and pushed him into the boat. I immediately pulled myself up and over the gunnels as if I were a 100-pound gymnast instead of a 220-pound, 35-year-old man who was cold and deeply concerned that a man-eating shark was waiting to bite my legs off.

I hugged Mike and Glenn. Mike was freezing and scared and embarrassed that he hadn't listened to me about the oar. I hugged them several more times before easy breathing returned. I turned the boat around and headed for home.

Our survival on that cold, wintry day happened through the goodness of the Lord, the protection of Saint Christopher (who is on the chain around my neck since 1950), and because Glenn Powers, a ten-year-old boy, knew instinctively how to handle an emergency on the Matanzas River.

Mike wasn't punished by me or Mindy. I didn't say too much to him because I was so happy that he was alive. He knew we were lucky, and so did I. Blessed is a better description.

Maybe that incident in the ancient city where he was born helped him cope during his twenty years of honorable military service in the U.S. Navy. Mike lived forty-six more great years before dying from esophageal cancer.

Thank you, God, and St. Christopher for protecting Mike and me that day and for watching over us all our

MINORCAN GUMBO FOR THE SOUL

days. Thank you, Glenn Powers, for being my young hero and having enough savvy to operate Papa's boat. Thank you, Papa Usina, for the special boat that saved your grandson.

This is a Billy Sanchez, plywood boat built in the 1950s. It's the one from which Mike had his first unintended swim in 1968. Papa Usina kept it at the St. Johns River cabin at Palmo Cove. We used it for skiing, fishing, hunting, and fun. We enjoyed it for more than 20 years.

Sweet Cindy, our oldest daughter, is perched on the rear gunnels in the photo. The 18-horsepower Johnson was a great engine. I started it by pulling the cord and steered it by moving the handle left or right. We controlled the speed by turning the throttle at the end of the handle. We lost the live bait well cover on a trip to St. Augustine, and I never built a new one.

The Copper-Topped Coffee Table and Its People

ON THE UNDERSIDE of the copper-topped coffee table in our family room are stenciled the words, "MonteCeito, Brown-Saltman, Los Angeles, Ca. 190-A." This special table is eight-sided and of very sturdy dark oak. The legs are turned with carved square rails between each leg. A heavy gauge sheet of copper covers the top and two inches down the sides, with brass tacks hammered in the same octagonal pattern in several rows on the top. It is strong enough for a 300-pound man to stand on and change a light bulb. It's also just the perfect height for toddlers who want to color, or slide race cars around and in-between the brass tacks, or sit on it and watch television while putting on shoes.

Reading the small amount of information described on the bottom of the table, we speculate its life's journey began at a furniture factory in California. Because of its low number, it might have been one of their early pieces. It is in the California Monterey or Mission style that was popular in the 1930s.

Phyllis and Charlie Usina, my wonderful in-laws, were the first owners of the table in about 1934 and it came to us as a gift from them.

Louise Wise Lewis Francis and her husband, Fred, were among the Usina's closest friends. Louise was the niece of FEC Railroad pioneer, Henry Flagler. She married Freddie Francis, a popular St. Augustine athlete and entrepreneur who owned a semi-pro baseball team. When you drive toward the city from St. Augustine on Ponce de Leon Boulevard, turn left toward the Fort and Francis Field is on the southern side of the street. It has been used for baseball since the 1920s and many a North City boy got his first chance to swing at a fast pitch on this old field.

Fred and Louise never had any children so "aunt" Louise sort of adopted Phyllis and Charlie Usina and lavished wonderful trips and gifts on their small family. Phyllis was a reporter for the *St. Augustine Record* at different times during this period, earning $21 per week. Charlie and his partner, W.I. Drysdale, were trying to create a successful business venture. They had tried a cocktail lounge (Dryz & Charlie's) and a men's clothing store (CharlesDales). Buying and operating the St. Augustine Alligator Farm was where they finally

THE COPPER-TOPPED COFFEE TABLE AND ITS PEOPLE

succeeded in the right business.

There were several small cottages at the Villa Flora Hotel on South St. George Street. Mimi and Papa moved there to have more room for their first child. Aunt Louise furnished the cottage as a present for the arrival of that child. This is why Malinda <u>Louise</u> Usina was the perfect name for this precious little girl who came smiling into the world on January 12, 1935.

The stunning copper-topped table we now have was one of the pieces Aunt Louise gave the Usinas. There was also dining and living room furniture and a dark red leather chair with the same kind of brass tacks as on the table.

The table was so unusual that it's one of the things Malinda remembers all through her childhood in the 1940s as an integral part of their household. This was quite a feat for her to remember because the Usina family moved almost every two years. At some point in a move to a more formal and traditional home, Mimi decided that the furniture and copper-topped table were dated, so they were put in storage.

Several houses later in the 1950s, all of the California furniture was retrieved and placed in their new house on Comares Avenue. After they moved from Comares Avenue, the copper-topped table ended up at Papa's office at the Alligator Farm. It was usually piled high with construction plans, magazines, trinkets for the gift shop, and soda pop bottles.

MINORCAN GUMBO FOR THE SOUL

In 1960, Mindy scoped out the table and, of course, convinced Papa that she needed it for our house at 12 D'Ayllon Street on Davis Shores. So, he gave it to us. We finally had a family room, and "Old Coppertop" became the centerpiece. Besides being beautiful and well-made, it was the only nice piece of furniture we possessed. We kept it shined and tried to keep the four kids from using it as a jumping off place and for hammering practice. But that was a fruitless effort.

It's always held a magical attraction for kids. It was here that Old Coppertop received mysterious little holes in it that look like someone wasn't satisfied while hammering on it unless a real nail was used. We will never know, and we really do not care anymore, as the holes add to the lore of the piece. One of the children who lived at 12 D'Ayllon will someday tell the story of the nail holes. Or not.

Many a night, Old Coppertop was used for Jaycee work. We could spread out lots of papers on it. When Tex and Marge Reardon lived across the street, Jaycee work was our life. Tex was president of the St. Augustine Jaycees and I was vice president. In 1961 the Jones were in charge of Records and Recognition for the St. Augustine Jaycees. Every project completed by our chapter was documented on forms provided by the state organization.

Mindy had a portable Royal typewriter that fit inside a carrying case. She dutifully typed all of the forms and records. The typewriter had a blue tape so all reports were sent in to headquarters with blue ink. Old Coppertop was part of all of this because the materials, forms, and pictures ended up on the table for collating into the project report forms. All of this hard work culminated with the St. Augustine Jaycees being named the best club in the State of Florida and one of the best ten in the United States when I was president. As a prize, I won a trip to Las Vegas for the national convention and was offered a job to manage internal affairs as a member of the staff of the U.S. Jaycees.

In August of 1963, Old Coppertop was stacked inside a moving van and shipped to Tulsa, Oklahoma; the national headquarters of the U.S. Jaycees. It was the first time the table left Florida, but it wouldn't be the last.

When we were ready to leave with the table for Oklahoma, Papa Usina wasn't standing in the driveway as Mindy, Bobby, Mike, Cindy, Laurie, and baby Mark (five months old at that time) started the two-day drive. But sweet Mimi and Cathy performed a Rockette-style kick and sang, "Always leave them laughing when you go." Nobody was laughing. There were tears aplenty, as our young family headed slowly out the Oneida Street house's iron gates in our 1959 VW bus loaded with most of our worldly goods.

As we left the house, we looked back, and there was Papa, by himself standing under a giant oak tree with his handkerchief in his hand, shedding tears. His precious

◄ **MINORCAN GUMBO FOR THE SOUL**

Malinda and all of his grandkids were leaving Florida for the Wild West with no plans to return anytime soon.

Malinda and I didn't know how devastated he and Mimi must have been, but as grandparents and great-grandparents, we now understand their deep sadness.

In Tulsa, Oklahoma, Old Coppertop resided in the living room of a modest rental house bordering a large ranch occupied by hundreds of humongous longhorn steers who came right up to our back fence and scared the dickens out of the little ones. We were living here when President John F. Kennedy was assassinated in Dallas on November 22, 1963. This was a sad day for us, the nation, and the world.

Old Coppertop had an interesting metamorphosis in Oklahoma. We noticed after a few months that the brass started to wrinkle, and the copper rose up in a very strange fashion. Alarmed, Malinda called a cabinet-maker to find out why. He said it was the result of the table being moved from a damp climate to a very dry one, which caused shrinking and made the copper top buckle. After Old Coppertop made its way back to Florida, the wood expanded again, and most of the wrinkles disappeared. The ones that remain remind us of our Jaycee days in Tulsa.

In June of 1964, Old Coppertop moved to Houston, Texas, for about a month. That was long enough for the Jones to completely understand that Houston, Texas was not where we wanted to stay for another day of our lives.

Unknown to us at the time, Papa was working on

plans to get his sweet Malinda and grandchildren back to Florida. When I heard about the prospect for a new job, I drove Mindy, Mike, Cindy, Laurie, Mark, and Nanny back to St. Augustine. Nanny had come to Texas to see everyone, and she jokingly told Papa that it took her to bring the grandchildren back home.

After leaving the family in St. Augustine, I flew back to Houston the next day and loaded our furniture, including Old Coppertop, into a large rental truck. I drove straight through from the Congress Inn Motel on Katy Road in Houston to St. Augustine Beach because I didn't have enough money to stay in a motel.

I arrived back in St. Augustine with $2.00 and a Gulf credit card that I used for gas and snacks. Old Coppertop was mighty glad to return to Florida, and so were the Nanny Jones and Mimi & Papa Usina families.

In July of 1964, I was selected executive director of Southeastern Fisheries Association. Old Coppertop and the rest of our belongings again went inside the rental truck and this time was driven to Tallahassee, Florida. We unloaded our goods at 2912 Harwood Street, a brand new house that Sy Deeb made available to us for no down payment as a courtesy to Representative Charlie Usina.

The table was quite prominent in the living area because our new home was less than 1,000 square feet. The kids played on, under, and around the table, but most of the time, it made a great footrest because the living room was so tiny that the couch and two chairs fit snugly up to Old Coppertop.

Not long after we arrived in Tallahassee, surprise, surprise, we were expecting again. Son Matthew was born on May 14, 1965.

Then, in December of 1965, Papa Usina's cancer was discovered. The Jones family drove to St. Augustine every weekend until he died on May 31, 1966. A major figure in our lives was gone. He was a fine man and missed greatly by everyone who knew him. Papa Usina is still strong in our thoughts, hearts, and prayers, and he always will be.

In 1967, Old Coppertop moved to 1109 Sandringham Drive in Tallahassee. After I built a family room on the back of the house in 1968, it sat in front of the old brick fireplace I created and was once again a jumping off platform and served as a nice book holder when Cindy or Laurie wanted to sit on the floor in front of a warm fire to read or finish a homework project.

Phyllis "Mimi" Usina moved to Tallahassee two years after Papa died and bought an older house on McDaniel Street. It was close enough for her to drive to the Jones' house on Sandringham almost every night for supper and conversation.

Then, in 1971, Mimi died after a 35-year battle with cancer. She was a courageous fighter and a classy lady, who was loved very much by her family and friends. She will also always be in our hearts and prayers. I still shed a joyful tear when I hear an old style pianist play a smooth rendition of "Poor Butterfly," a song Mimi played for me anytime I found her at or near a piano. Her left hand had a magical way of making the melody in the right hand come to life. I don't recall ever seeing her use a printed sheet of music. If you could hum it, she could play it with great fervor.

In 1972, we moved to 1121 Lasswade Drive in Tallahassee, which was the favorite of all the Jones family houses. It had a large pool gently placed in a beautifully landscaped backyard and a large fireplace in the family room where Old Coppertop silently sat. Many fun conversations with friends and family took place sitting in front of the fireplace with our feet propped up on Old Coppertop.

The kids were mostly grown (or thought they were) by this time. Instead of race cars or books on the table, a parental unit would often find ring marks where a glass with some kind of alcohol concoction had been placed for too long. One good thing about copper though, is that with strong muscles and lots of Brasso, most of the rings and discolorations could be removed. Of course, the punched holes and initials are there for the duration, and that's a good thing!

In 1985 the table moved to 312 East Georgia Street and stood in a place of prominence in the upstairs living area where it welcomed all of our new grandchildren for the next twelve years. Old Coppertop wasn't finished

MINORCAN GUMBO FOR THE SOUL

with its journey yet!

In 1996, the Georgia Street home/office was sold, and we moved in 1996 to a rental apartment at what our family termed the "Terrace Street Plantation." Our "plantation home" was the only place we ever lived where you could lie in bed and get a snack out of the kitchen without getting out of bed. It was very small! We didn't stay there long, and Old Coppertop was about ready to take a long trip north.

When we purchased a new townhouse at Pink Flamingo Lane in Tallahassee, Malinda wanted a more formal coffee table, so Old Coppertop headed for Banner Elk in the North Carolina mountains. It arrived at 499 Puckett Road in February 1997 while Bill Berry and his boys, Todd and Brent, were putting the finishing touches on our little log cabin.

Lily Cat Jones

THE COPPER-TOPPED COFFEE TABLE AND ITS PEOPLE ⤴

Old Coppertop stayed in front of the fireplace Sonny Burchfield and I built until 2016 when we sold the cabin. It's now back in Tallahassee in the living room of our home in Waverly Hills and will be until we are called home. Where the table will end up is anyone's guess, but I thought readers might enjoy this historical story about how one piece of furniture touched so many lives and created an interesting story on its own.

What stories it could tell if it could only talk.

The Inheritance

I WANTED TO write something about the fishing pole my dad gave me just before he died. I consider it my inheritance, but when you think about an inheritance it's so much more than a single object.

My father, Robert H. Jones, Jr., was born in Titusville, Florida, on October 2, 1913, and left this earth from Jacksonville, Florida, on August 18, 1996. My grandfather, Robert H. Jones, Sr., was a commercial fisherman in Titusville during his adult life, according to U.S. Census Reports. He was married to Lillian S. Knowles. Surely, my love of the ocean and Florida's wilderness as a 6th generation Floridian comes from my ancestors. I thank them very much for that.

My father and his brother, Louis, and sister, Edith, were raised by their Aunt Maude Poppell in Titusville. Maude may have been Lillian's sister.

My grandmother died when she was twenty-five years old in 1919. My father was three years old at the

THE INHERITANCE

time of her death. Grandfather Jones must have been devastated to lose his wife at such a young age. The only time my mother, Mary Frances Brinson Jones, met my grandfather was when she and Bob Jr. were on a date in 1932. Grandfather Jones came out the back door from the kitchen of the restaurant where he worked as a dishwasher to say hello and shake her hand.

Grandfather Jones was a heavy drinker according to anecdotal information that my brother, Ray, and sister, Robin, have discerned over the years. They were told that one night he was so drunk that he passed out on the FEC railroad tracks, and a train ran over him. I hope to confirm that story or learn the truth one of these days. If that is the way he died, it was a sad ending indeed to what sounds like a sad life. May he rest in peace.

In all the years I knew my father, he never mentioned his father. Maybe the hurt was too painful to dredge up, or maybe he couldn't bring himself to forgive his father for leaving, causing the kids to be raised by his sister-in-law.

Daddy left my mother, me, and my brother and sister in 1944, so I never got to know the Titusville family. I did see Uncle Louis once, during WWII when he came to St. Augustine all spiffy in his Army uniform. We all went to the Fort Green and took pictures with an old Kodak box camera.

I met Aunt Edith once on a trip to her house when I was very young. I remember lots of people going to a silent movie uptown and listening to a piano player add melodrama to the movie with his music.

Chances are my father and his siblings didn't inherit anything from their father but a chance to live and experience some real hard times. My father was a survivor of the WWI, the Hoover Days, the Great Depression, WWII, and the Korean and Vietnam Wars. He spent time in 1985 in Vietnam as a contract mechanic and might have gotten married over there to add to the experience of having about eight wives during his lifetime.

Robert H. Jones, Jr. and Mary Frances Brinson had three children. I am the oldest, Richard was the middle child, and Lesta Ann is the youngest. I had always thought I was the first born. But while I was first born to Mary Frances, I was not first born to Robert.

When I was about forty-five years old, there was an interesting article in the *Florida Times Union* about a daughter who finally found her dad after searching for him for decades. It turned out that her dad was also my dad, but she was a year older than I. Evidently Daddy Jones played around a bit too much, but his lover didn't want him to know she was pregnant. He never knew he had fathered another child until he received that strange phone call one afternoon from the daughter he never knew he had. I didn't get a chance to meet her, but I would have liked to have said hello.

Daddy and Mama divorced in 1944. Shortly thereafter, Mama drove us to Miami to live with William and Bernice

THE INHERITANCE

Carey at 857 NW 21st Terrace. We didn't see Daddy very much during the war years. I do remember him coming down once and taking us to Crandon Park, where we climbed in the big curvy trees and rode ponies. We were glad to see him since we didn't fully understand the toll of the divorce on Mama. She never complained about raising her three children on guts and love, but she never had many good things to say about Daddy.

We saw him more when we moved back to St. Augustine in 1947. We lived thirty-five miles from his house. I remember spending several weeks during the summer with him and with his second wife, Kathleen. They had five great kids together and lived in a two-bedroom apartment on Jacksonville Southside. Kathleen was very nice to me and I loved her, but did not tell Mama.

Daddy worked at a Gulf Station on San Marco Boulevard and Lasalle Streets in Jacksonville and eventually became a partner at Koenig & Jones service station. He was a very hard worker and could fix any kind of car problem. He accomplished a lot for someone with less than an eighth grade education.

Eventually, Daddy divorced Kathleen and married several other women during his life. He was married to a 40-year-old Filipino lady when he died August 18, 1996 at the age of 82.

Before his death, I often visited the gas station where Daddy worked when I traveled in the Jacksonville area on fish business. In his later years, he usually called Kathleen and put her on the phone for me to say hello and chat for a minute. For some reason, Daddy had a very cordial relationship with Kathleen and their children after their divorce.

The last place I visited him was on Beach Boulevard which was maybe three or four miles east of I-95. I brought him fish or shrimp every once in a while, which always made him smile. I knew he was glad to see me. I was glad to see him also, but many times, I thought about how different things might have been if he hadn't left us. I only wondered for a few minutes, though, because I wouldn't change one thing in my life that would have prevented me falling in love with and marrying Malinda Louise Usina and having five wonderful children who created life for so many others.

The important thing was Daddy and I had a very peaceful adult relationship. I don't ever recall a harsh word or even the hint of an argument between us. Maybe it was because we both came to recognize each other as the men we had become. He was always in a good mood when I visited him and seemed sad when I drove away. He always asked about Mindy and the kids, as well as Mama and Aunt Pat.

Daddy finally quit working on cars when he hit seventy-nine or eighty. He couldn't get off the creeper one day after working on his back underneath a car. It was

THE INHERITANCE

great that he was able to work for sixty years in an occupation he loved and knew so well.

During the last year of Daddy's life when he was very sick, I saw him five or six times. I thought about him often, as I knew his time was coming to an end. It was on the next to the last time I saw him alive that he gave me his favorite fishing rod and reel. I recognized the pole because he used it when the two of us met a couple of times at Usina's Fish Camp on Vilano Beach many years earlier. I took him fishing in a 14-foot Billy Sanchez-built wooden boat powered by a mighty 18-HP Johnson outboard motor that had belonged to Mindy's dad.

I might have had Mike with me, but I can't remember. I do remember Daddy using a heavy, short, stout fishing pole because he was a meat fisherman. He wanted to catch fish to take home and cook, and he was very good at it. He loved to catch and eat fish.

One of my first and favorite memories of him is throwing a cast net on St. Augustine Beach and catching croaker sacks full of ocean mullet. That was about 1938. I imagine Daddy probably caught over a thousand fish with this pole during his lifetime. It turned out that this rod and reel was my inheritance from my father.

Some people might think that's not much of an inheritance. Well, first of all, Daddy and Mary Frances Brinson Jones, through the grace of God, gave me life, which put me in the hunt to do all I am capable of doing during my short journey. Without that life, what would have happened to Mindy, Michael, Cynthia, Laurie, Mark, Matthew, and all of their kids and grandkids? Robert H. and Mary Frances gave me the genes that have sustained a heavy frame my entire life, allowing my big body to be healthy. He and Mary Frances gave me a good sense of humor and the innate ability to always believe everything is going to turn out okay.

So, my inheritance is bountiful when you think about it. And I have Daddy's fishing pole to use and look at whenever I wish. That makes me glad, not sad.

The Chairs

ONCE UPON A time in the Land of Florida were two special but ordinary looking chairs. They were built with solid native cypress lumber and held tightly together by glue and galvanized nails. The wood came from trees in St. Augustine and this made the chairs proud. They had countless coats of paint of myriad colors that changed their outside appearance during the many years they moved from place to place. As they grew older, a heavy coat of high gloss white paint was the easiest to maintain. It was amazing to watch them perk up after their fresh coat of paint each year. They preferred being painted in the spring because their greatest use was during the following summer and fall.

Animals and humans alike enjoyed the chairs. They are a happy place for grandchildren to sit after getting tired and sweaty from climbing trees and running around the hilly backyard. They are home to three families of gray squirrels, and majestic red-tailed hawks often perched on the arms while searching for prey. Once a hawk swooped down from one of the chairs and caught a black snake. Multiple families of redbirds have perched on the chairs to rest from their never-ending feeding obligations to their young babies tucked safely away in their nests.

The chairs were so similar it was difficult to tell them apart except that one was a little bigger. The chairs were created a few years apart. "Big Chair" had a few more dings and scrapes received at different places he lived before joining "Little Chair" for life. After they became chair mates, they took great pride in caring for each other. If ever there were two chairs meant to be together, this was the pair.

THE CHAIRS

There were a few times when the chairs gazed in the opposite direction. They assumed this position to protect each other from the blind side when heavy drama was in abundance. They also took this position every now and then in their younger years when they had a spat.

They were forever bonded. The thought of these chairs separating was a non-issue, but youthful attitudes and struggling circumstances caused some heated discussions. Most of the time, arguments started because of Big Chair's temper. Even though Little Chair's character and her grit were just as strong as or stronger than Big Chair's, Little Chair did not like to argue. However, Little Chair was relentless, especially when she knew she was right. That was most of the time.

Big Chair didn't have an inquisitive nature. He

missed many things swirling around their existence. He felt things would always work out, so it wasn't necessary to interfere or control everything. On the other hand, Little Chair could ask twenty questions on any subject before a person could say "Tallahassee."

The disagreements between Big Chair and Little Chair never lasted long and never impacted their love or respect for each other. They quickly were back looking at each other, deciding how to resolve any problems. The night never passed unless all conflicts were resolved.

The special times of quiet talking, close up and deeply personal, were some of the best moments of their lives. It was understood that neither chair would knowingly, or purposefully, hurt the other. Chair mates know this.

THE CHAIRS

Soulmates know this, too.

Chairs need to pick and choose the words they say in anger very carefully. Words spoken in anger by someone you love, and who loves you, are the words that hurt the most and are the most difficult (if not impossible) to take back. Sometimes, jealousy makes us say and do things we shouldn't. Big Chair and Little Chair learned long ago that if you are ever hurt and don't know what to do, ask someone you love to listen to what happened.

There used to be five small chairs in this group, but they moved away to find their own backyard. When the five chairs were young and happy, it was the best time in the world for Big Chair and Little Chair.

The chairs always moved down the same path. They swapped places at times with Little Chair in charge. Their path continued in the same direction no matter which chair had the lead. *Right is right and wrong is wrong.* These seven words are simple to say, but a life's work to obey by thoughts, words, and deeds.

There is a Big Backyard over the horizon with all kinds, sizes and shapes of trees. The colors of the birds are too many to count. The softness of their songs takes your breath away. The emerald green grass is so thick and shiny it looks and feels like a velvet rug. The cool summer winds move gently across the Big Backyard, making the grass shimmy back and forth in a melodic dance. Watching the grass ripple back and forth as far as the eye can see evokes a euphoric feeling of peace.

Children run and play with utter joy in the Big Backyard. There are ten thousand swing sets and seesaws. There are triple sliding boards with five and six hairpin turns. There are lemonade stands, popcorn carts, hot dogs, cotton candy, and chocolate cookies waiting for anyone to eat from the longest picnic table ever built. There are millions of chairs in all shades of color in the Big Backyard.

Big Chair and Little Chair are content in their present backyard. They hope to remain there for many more years. They accept and cherish the day they move to the Big Backyard.

THE CHAIRS

In the Big Backyard, there are chairs that were part of our group many years ago. They expected arrival of Big Chair and Little Chair. There are fancy chairs under colorful awnings protecting their sensitive nature. There are iron chairs tough enough to survive trials and trauma in any yards where they were placed. The Big Backyard welcomes all chairs that did what they were created for.

The Big Backyard is there for everyone. There is no limit to the number of chairs that will be welcomed. Each chair makes its own decisions and is judged by the Master Gardener, accordingly. The Master Gardener is very wise, loving, and full of forgiveness.

There will come a time when one of the chairs will

no longer be able to serve the purpose for which it was created. No chair knows when that time will come, but it will come. Whichever chair turns over and goes to the Big Backyard first, the chair mate left will be sustained by happy memories until it's time to move to the Big Backyard.

At the appointed time the other chair will fall over and complete its purpose. It will join the other chairs in the Big Backyard - for eternity.

If these chairs are blessed, and I'm sure they are, they will always be a sweet memory for those who knew and loved them.

It is not known for sure, but it's possible chairs take their love with them. Big Chair and Little Chair hope to

THE CHAIRS

be together in the Big Backyard under a shady, moss-laden oak tree during warm summer days saying, "Come sit with us - rest for a while - and we will make you smile."

Bucky Powers

ALLEN FREDERICK "BUCKY" Powers of St. Augustine, Florida, was a good young man and will be a fine old man whenever he decides he is old. I heard about Bucky Powers long before he knew I was anything other than a North City kid living in the old house at the end of the dirt driveway behind P.J. Manucy's grocery store on San Marco Avenue across from Russell's Bar B Que.

Bucky was a handful during his youth. He didn't break any laws, but he bent the one concerning young folks drinking beer. Then again, so did all of the other boys and lots of the girls in that era.

He was tough, with a high tolerance for pain, and he worked hard as a plumber apprentice during every summer in high school to stay in top shape. He played football at Ketterlinus High School, which usually competed for the conference championship. He hung out with some of the biggest and rowdiest boys in town who spent evenings with their girls at Black Point, Russell's Drive-In, or roaming the town in their homemade 1936-1941 dune buggies.

Many were gifted athletes and all were world-class beer drinkers. There is no telling how well some of them could have played college football if they had concentrated on athletics instead of living for the fruits of joy and pleasure they tried to gather each day and night.

Bucky Powers at the plate. Red Cox the umpire.

When Bucky was in his heyday at Ketterlinus, odd things happened every now and then to the tall palm trees surrounding the gardens at the west end of the Bridge of Lions. The tops of the palm trees would be burned. Someone apparently climbed the tree and set them on fire, then raced across the bridge to park along the Davis

◄ MINORCAN GUMBO FOR THE SOUL

Shores seawall to see how long it took for the fire trucks to arrive. Those dark parking places provided a good view of the flaming and flickering palms. Bucky wouldn't have done anything like that, but I'm not too sure about some of his friends. There was another Bucky about the same age who was a bit of a hellraiser, but I won't mention his last name.

Another phenomenon that drove city officials and policemen wild was the mysterious "rolling cannonballs." Someone would remove an iron cannon ball from its stack near the ancient howitzer on Bay Street, lug the heavy iron ball to the middle of the bridge, and let the ball roll noisily down Cathedral Street. To my knowledge, nobody was ever injured, but that was either a miracle or because the event happened after 11:00 p.m., when the sidewalks were "rolled up for the evening." Bucky was never caught or formally accused as far as I know, but someday I will ask him if he knows anything about these bayside mysteries. After this happened quite a few times, the city welded the cannonballs together so that they could no longer be removed. That was a wise decision by the city fathers.

None of my St. Joseph Academy High School buddies had a car or even thought much about when they might get one. The "gang" would walk up San Marco Avenue through the ancient coquina city cates, arriving at the iron rail fence in front of the Episcopalian Church on the corner of King Street. There, we perched on the cold rail, lit up our Marlboros and watched girls and small town life pass by us from dark until 10:00 p.m. We liked the nightly ritual of sitting and standing on the corner, but we had no comprehension of how this wonderful, carefree 1950s life was slipping away day by day.

When Bucky and his friends came by, we were awed by the loud, baritone mufflers on cars and amazed by their speed as they raced down King Street on the way to the beach for a party. They ignored us, of course, as we were just the "St. Joe boys." In our minds, they were really living. Bucky and his friends had a car, beer, and beautiful girls who liked to party. They were the Fonzis of our town, except, of course, the Fonz had not been created in 1950.

"What a life Bucky and his friends are having!" we thought as we sat our young butts on that cold steel rail fence and waited for Fabian Funk to make nightly runs in his old Plymouth taxi cab. The KHS boys were living the dream we could only imagine.

The most exciting thing we did back then was go skinny dipping in the Clay Hole off Mill Creek Road (F. Charles Usina Highway now) or steal an orange or grapefruit from Mulligan's Orange Stand on the way home late at night.

Bucky's mom was a quiet, God-fearing lady working hard to raise a house full of kids. Bucky's dad was very gruff. He was tough as nails and seemed serious the few times I saw him. He grew up hard like the rest of his contemporaries, was a hard worker, and knew the value of having a job at the Miller Shops locomotive facility north of town. He knew my grandfather, Philip Patrick Brinson, who was an engineer for the Florida East Coast railroad. My mother told me that Mr. Powers visited my grandfather, who had become blind. I'm told they spent wonderful times sitting in the front porch rocking chairs, reminiscing about their experiences in the golden days working on Mr. Flagler's railroad. Mama said Mr. Powers was always friendly to her and Aunt Pat, and they enjoyed his visits at 146 Cunningham Drive.

Bucky finished high school all in one piece and shortly thereafter, he joined the USAF, serving with honor in the Korean War. He spent over a year in Korea and told me that the worst injury he got while he was there was a broken jaw. He said, "I was in a bar, drinking a glass of milk or something like that, and someone threw a punch at my buddy who ducked, leaving me to get my clock cleaned for no reason at all." I have to believe this is true, for to my knowledge Bucky has never lied to me. Bucky served in a combat zone while in Korea, and for that, and many other reasons, will always have a special place in my heart.

After high school and honorable military service, Bucky started dating Nancy Trask, one of my dear under-classmates and friends. He started working for Ginty's Plumbing along with his brother, Ralph, also one of my heroes. Ralph was part of the Normandy Invasion in World War II and an honorable member of the greatest generation.

We water-skied and partied quite often, and like the old song says, "we always had a mighty fine time." We were not heavy drinkers, but on the weekends, we took our pint bottles of Canadian Club or Old Mr. Boston or whatever we could afford and went to someone's house to listen to music, dance, eat, talk, play games, and just have fun. The bond of friendship between our families has never stopped growing.

Bucky and Nancy were married a few months after us in 1955. They lived upstairs above Nancy's parents in a small apartment for the first few years because they were saving all of their money to build their first love nest.

On one occasion, which Bucky wishes I would forget, we had been dancing and partying at Surfside Casino on Vilano Beach. Bucky had one or two more drinks in his system than it could stand. As a result, he couldn't walk straight, so I had to horse him down the stairs at Surfside, get him in the car, and take him and Nancy home. Nancy was pregnant, so that delicate condition added more drama to the scene that followed.

Mindy was in the backseat with Nancy. Bucky was in the front seat with me. As we slowly cruised up San

MINORCAN GUMBO FOR THE SOUL

Marco Avenue near Kentucky Jim's Liquor Store, Bucky said, "Stop, I gotta pee."

I told him, "Wait 'til you get home; it's only a couple of minutes away."

"I gotta pee *now*," he responded.

I pulled up to the curb so he could use Kentucky Jim's bathroom at the rear of the store. Bucky jumped out of the car before it completely stopped and whizzed right there in the gutter on San Marco Avenue. Nancy was about to have a hissy fit, and Mindy was bent over in hysterics. It was sort of funny to see a grown man turn toward a car full of laughing people with such a happy and relieved smile on his face. He was oblivious to his surroundings. We were not!

Thank God Bucky was always a kind and gentle drinker. If he had been a mean drinker with the strength of a gorilla it would have been a nightmare for all concerned. Thinking back, he might have ended up with more broken bones than he's had from legitimate accidents, or I might have been the one with the broken bones.

I shoved Bucky back into the car, stepped around to the driver's side, then slammed it in low gear. I drove them to his in-laws, Ray and Edith Trask, where they were living. Once we got into the house, I planned to sneak him up the stairs to their bedroom. My effort to move him upward was among the most frustrating chores I have ever had. About halfway up the stairs, he decided he didn't want to go any further. There we all were – Nancy, (pregnant) Mindy (who was about to burst with laughter), me (worried), and a reluctant man who didn't want to finish the climb up the stairs and fall into his bed.

Bucky was having a difficult time figuring out where he was and where he was going. Somehow I managed to get him to the top of the stairs. He must have decided to let me take him the last few steps because it would have taken two or more strong guys to take him against his will. We left them in their room and went home to our tiny apartment at 22 Central Avenue, chuckling all the way at what this episode will look like to a reader of a short story (Sorry, Bucky).

Mindy called Nancy the next day and asked how everything went the rest of the evening.

Nancy said, "He got sick later that night and didn't want to mess up the carpet, so he opened the top dresser drawer and did his thing all over my night clothes."

I don't know what Nancy said to him, but she sure got his attention. I never had to take him home again from any party, ever.

Because Cindy was on the way and we only had one bedroom at our Wolfe Apartments, a few months later, we moved to 66 Coquina Street. Our little concrete block house backed up to Bucky's new home on Arricola Avenue. It was a short walk through the backyards to get to Bucky's. It was easy for him to get to our house to unplug the toilet that was routinely stopped up because another cloth diaper had slipped out of someone's hand during the process of changing diapers.

Bucky and I were still in the building trade in 1960. I was working for myself some of the time, and Bucky was still with Ginty's, working for Ian Wainwright. Bucky left the trade a few years later to organize a St. Johns County Building Department. After a very successful stint and this job he ran for, he was elected property appraiser for the remainder of his working years.

We stayed in touch throughout the next four decades and spent many days and evenings together during the summer time. We fished, water-skied, and concentrated on raising our families. We did many things on the waters of St. Johns County as families.

One outing I remember well was when six of us went on a floundering fishing trip in my 17-foot Bonita fishing boat. The crew consisted of Bucky and Nancy, Sonny and Phyllis Burchfield, and Mindy and me. We met at Bucky's house on Anastasia Island because the boat was easy to launch from the Lighthouse Park ramp. It also had a safer walkway for the ladies to get aboard the boat without slipping down. We had flounder gigs, a battery for the underwater lights, blankets, and more than an adequate supply of frozen daiquiris. We needed the daq's, as it was a balmy summer evening in the Oldest City and we did not want to become dehydrated.

A good time to gig a flounder is when the tide is calm on a moonless evening. We loaded ourselves and a mountain of gear into the boat. The Evinrude motor cranked immediately when I pushed the switch, then we started across the Bay to the sandbar that runs north and south a couple of hundred yards east of the Fort. No matter how hard I tried, because of its weight, I couldn't get the boat on a plane as we moved out into Salt Run . We still made good time going past the marina and around the northern tip of Davis Shores. At that point, all of the sparkling lights and skyline of St. Augustine came into view. The almost ancient Bridge of Lions is a wonderful sight to behold at night, with all its lights glowing and creating wavy reflections on the bay.

We cut across Matanzas Bay in a straight line toward the shadows and outline of the Castillo de San Marcos. All of us knew the bay like the backs of our hands so we were never in any danger of getting lost. Any of us could find the channel flowing alongside the Fort with a blindfold on.

We crossed the open waters without any major incidents. Ten minutes later, we reached the spot to begin our quest for the elusive, but delicious, Florida flounder. Bucky loudly said, "Be as quiet as possible to avoid spooking any flounder resting nearby."

Imagine getting six people, some of them partially

inebriated, out of the high-sided boat into the mud along the channel on a pitch black night. Sonny hooked up the underwater lights to the battery, we all put on life preservers, and finally decided what kind of skirmish line we were going to walk along the shoreline. It reminded me very much of a Chinese fire drill gone awry.

The girls weren't particularly excited about stepping out of the warm environment in the boat into the cold, dark water where there might be oozing mud, pinching crabs, stingrays, or worse. Nobody was quiet, and as if on cue, the giggling started when we tried to form a straight line to walk down the creek. Of course, the ladies walked in the shallow water, and the men got the deeper water ... except Sonny, who was pulling the inner tube with the battery hooked up to the underwater lights.

It could have been Bucky, or it might have been Malinda who observed that with all the noise coming from our motley crew, the flounders had all probably risen from the bottom and extended their heads above the surface to see what in the world was going on. It was a very noisy outing, and I didn't expect us to actually gig a flounder.

It really didn't matter because the experience was worthwhile just being out in a boat late at night while the babysitters watched over the little ones. When I think back on that evening, it actually was a lot easier than putting two, three, or four little ones to bed.

Nevertheless, the flounder goddess was with us that evening. All of a sudden, Malinda said, "I think I see one!" Down went the gig with all her might into the fishy-looking form in the mud, and then, all hell broke loose. Mindy gigged a giant seven-pound flounder that was not happy with a steel spike through its head or the screaming lady pushing down excitedly at the other end. The big flounder kicked up enough water to completely soak Malinda and whoever reached down and slid his hand under the flounder to pick it up (probably Sonny Burchfield).

A mighty roar came forth from the crew, echoing across the marsh grass into the pricey homes on Water Street. The men looked at each other with a puzzled expression, wondering how a girl gigged the biggest flounder seen in a long time. Nothing was said, though, because there was no way to change the outcome of the evening. The Minorcan Queen ruled in all her glory. Rightfully so.

That was the only fish gigged that night. As I recall, it was stuffed with crabmeat dressing, baked and served to the crew a few nights later. The memorable evening started at Bucky and Nancy's and finished with the flounder dinner there.

Bucky also had a boat, but just the thought of putting that much equipment plus daiquiris and fried chicken in his boat was unthinkable. It was common knowledge in St. Augustine that "you never ate fried chicken or any food item while in the Powers' boat." Bucky has always been very fastidious. Cleanliness is not an option with Bucky; it is a lifestyle. While some might call it picky, I was always comfortable knowing if a piece of food dropped on the floor at Bucky's house, you could pick it up and eat it without fear of any bacteria.

Bucky and Nancy came to Tallahassee at least once a year after the 1970s for a fun-filled visit – usually an FSU football game or one of our kids' special performances at Leon High School. We often spent two weeks or more cleaning and painting just prior to their arrival because we knew we would get an inspection from old eagle eye.

When we were on Sandringham Drive, Mindy stayed on my case every day to get the painting finished, and I vividly recall just barely getting the eaves finished in time for one of their visits. I told Mindy, "Maybe it isn't worth having Bucky and Nancy come over if I'm going to have to work this hard every year!" She just laughed, and so did I. We loved their visits and looked forward to the annual "inspection."

In retaliation for the inspection, Mindy always had a small list of projects that were out of my league for Bucky to complete … or any other handy Minorcan who happened to come by the house.

Bucky and Nancy built a mountain house in North Carolina in 1986. They invited us for an annual trek of shopping, card playing, and eating. Over the next decade, as soon as the frost covered the pumpkins, we knew it was time for Valle Crucis and the Wooly Worm Festival in Banner Elk. Those were some of the most fun-filled years of our lives. It wasn't unusual for five or six couples to stay at the "Powers' Bed and Breakfast" from one night to a week or more.

Over the years, most of our friends built their own cabins in North Carolina, but nostalgia still reigns supreme when we all show up at the Powers for food and mirth – something we try to do on a regular basis. In all of these years, I can't recall a cross word spoken between us and Bucky and Nancy. That is not because we don't have differences of opinion and strong feelings about certain issues, but we have always given each other all the wiggle room needed for true friendship.

There have been some very tough times over the years raising kids. The toughest, of course, for Bucky and Nancy was middle son, Tommy's, fatal automobile crash. I gave the eulogy for Tommy at the request of the family, which was very difficult for me. It was not as hard as it pertains to Tommy, for he went to a better place where the hurts of life are soothed. The difficult part was looking at Bucky and Nancy and feeling their deep grief from losing a child they had raised and tried so hard to set on the right path. Tommy received unconditional love. Glen and Chris, Tommy's brothers, also received unconditional love and are wonderful sons and fathers. They give Bucky and Nancy great joy.

Bucky and Nancy are now in the grandparent mode, with Lindsey already graduated from the University of Florida and working fulltime. Although Bucky is retired, I would not change jobs with him. If he is retired, then God please help me work until the day before I'm taken home. It would be more accurate to say he is retired from the county, but his workload seems to grow exponentially with each passing day. And that is good. All we have to do is keep him off of the roof, if possible, but if he must go up the ladder, we pray that if he slips, he will land on the grass and not the concrete.

Bucky has come to a place in life where you can no longer do with your body what your mind thinks you can. Many of us are in that same place.

There are numerous other stories I could tell about my friend. More importantly, there are stories waiting to be lived and then told. I'm looking forward to being part of them. I love you, Bucky and Nancy Powers. I'm glad we have been friends for almost seven decades. God Bless.

Bobby Jones' First Prom

I LIVED AT Riverside Fish Camp on Vilano Beach the year I entered St. Joseph's Academy in September of 1948. The preceding year I was at Ketterlinus High School. Principal Doug Hartley called me into his office one morning after I'd missed a lot of school days and said I was expelled from KHS and had better mend my ways. Thinking back, I don't know any other friends expelled from high school. I didn't think I deserved it back then and I still don't.

Mama was distraught. Over the summer, unbeknownst to me, she contacted Father John W. Love, Pastor of Cathedral Parish. She asked him to help her oldest son and he agreed after hearing her plea. After the meeting, Mama told me I would be going to St. Joseph's Academy in September, and that her decision was final.

My God, what would I do around all those Catholics? I had never even seen a nun or priest up close, and now they would be my teachers. Most of my friends happened to be Catholics, but we never talked about religion. It turned out not so bad because some of my Vilano Beach buddies attended St. Joe and wanted me to come play football. I liked that. They also told me there were some beautiful girls at St. Joe. 'Nuff said.

It was May of 1949, and almost everyone had a date to the prom. I asked classmate and neighbor, Sally Reyes, to go with me and she said yes. Somehow I earned enough money or borrowed from my tuition money to buy her a big orchid corsage.

To say the Jones family didn't have a lot of money would be a gross understatement. I had a pair of black shoes, but I would probably have worn brown ones if that was all I had. I didn't have a car. I can't recall if Sally and I walked from North City to the Lyceum or whether her rough and tough daddy drove us. It was probably the latter. Mr. Vincent and Miss Minerva were wonderful parents to Sally.

We arrived at the St. Joe Lyceum early the evening of the prom all dolled up like the other kids. I think everyone in high school was there with or without dates because it was a school event. We walked into the darkened (but not too darkened because, remember, this was a Catholic school in the 1940s) and beautifully decorated gym to find a table with kids who were also in the ninth grade. We found one filled with familiar faces and they asked us to sit down. Thinking back we were probably given some strange looks, but nobody said anything as I recall.

Sally and I danced every dance, switching partners until we danced with everyone at the table. We all had a good time doing the jitterbug and slow dancing to songs like "Bewitched, Bothered and Bewildered."

At some point during the evening, it dawned on me that I wasn't dressed quite like everyone else. In fact, I was the only one there with white pants and a black coat instead of a white dinner jacket and black pants with a shiny, satin stripe down the sides.

Nanny couldn't afford to rent me a tux, so she borrowed some white pants from a friend. I think the black coat I wore was from a friend of the family who lost their uncle the previous year. I was probably wearing a dead man's jacket, but didn't know it.

I felt embarrassed for Sally being at the prom with an oddball. I felt embarrassed for Nanny, because she must have been chagrined that her son was going to the prom dressed the opposite of everybody else. I felt embarrassed but there was no place to hide. "Just suck it up and do the best you can" was all that was available.

In looking back on that evening sixty-eight years ago, maybe that's why I don't worry much about what people say; family and real friends accept you for what you are on the inside, not just what they can see on the outside.

Pollyanna Bobby then; Pollyanna Bobby now – just a man who chooses to be happy every day and in every way possible.

A Day Remembered In My Trade

MINDY HAD GOTTEN up first, as she always does, made the coffee, and was making breakfast by the time I came out of the bedroom ready for work. Many times, she had my two sandwiches ready, neatly wrapped in tinfoil and placed in the banged-up aluminum lunch box I used throughout my career as a bricklayer, plasterer, and cement finisher. After quickly eating breakfast I poured fresh coffee into the thermos, put it in the box, and was good to go until suppertime.

I was wearing a long-sleeved tee shirt under the heaviest sweatshirt I owned, and, on top, my red and black checkered winter jacket was buttoned all the way up to the neck. The broad woolen collar was turned up and resting on my FSU cap. I was wearing the oldest pair of faded jeans I owned. I plastered in them before, and once pants are used for plastering, they never look the same.

A DAY REMEMBERED IN MY TRADE

The noisy, nine-year-old heater near the floor of my dark green 1951 Chevrolet pickup truck was pumping out all the hot air it could manage. As hard as it worked, it wasn't enough to offer much help in reducing St. Augustine's bone chilling air that February morning in 1960.

Laurie, our third child, was on the way six months hence, and we really needed some money to pay our bills, buy food, and keep things going. I drove north from my house at 66 Coquina Drive, pulled out on A1A, crossed the Bridge of Lions to Ponce de Leon Boulevard, turned left on State Road 16, and continued west to the job site off the Mill Creek road.

Brick layers, cement finishers, and plasterers didn't wear gloves and never sat down to work. "Wussies wear gloves, and only shoemakers sit to work," was what the old-timers said any time their "rituals" were broken.

When I arrived at the concrete block house, a fire was roaring in the 55-gallon steel drum used to burn scraps of wood and paper left over from the construction. The sturdy steel drum had air vents cut near the bottom, allowing it to function like a monitor heater. Standing around the fire that morning were Sonny Burchfield, Drayton Pacetti, and Uncle Charlie Pacetti, who was, by far, the oldest in the group. Drayton was Sonny's father-in-law, and Uncle Charlie was his great uncle-in-law. These three men were vintage artisans who could build anything using masonry products. I was glad to work with them because they were picky about people with whom they shared a scaffold.

I parked away from the fire and lime box and joined the others who were warming themselves around the fire. My classic Chevy with those small, rounded pane windows on each side of the truck was originally owned by the San Marco Construction Company. After they got all they could from it for over 100,000 miles, they sold it. Papa Usina, my awesome father-in-law, bought it for $300 and during the next year, I paid him back. It was a beautiful truck with 4-inch split rims on all of the wheels. It had four nearly bald whitewall tires that made hauling scaffold boards or riding the dunes on St. Augustine and Vilano Beach easy and safe. It would turn out to be the prettiest truck I would ever own.

When I stepped out of the truck that morning in 1960, Uncle Charlie Pacetti said, "Morning, Trigger." It was around 7:15 a.m., and we were on the scaffold from 7:30 until noon, and again from 12:30 to 4:00 to get in our full eight-hour day. Our laborer was C.W. Major, a cheerful, always-smiling black man who easily took care of four plasterers or bricklayers. He could move scaffolds to the next room to be plastered, screen the lime, and have it piled up on the mortar board before we were ready to put the hardening agent into the mix. C.W. was a wonderful person with a fantastic work ethic. He was respected by all of the journeymen and people who worked with him

A DAY REMEMBERED IN MY TRADE

for more than twenty-five years. When I think of masonry work and the good people I have known, I always include C.W. Major.

When plastering a room the way we did it in the 1950s and 1960s, the first coat (brown coat) was applied from the baseboard to about six feet high. The scaffold was then set up, and the top of the walls and ceilings were given their portion of the brown coat. Straight edges and Darbies, made from straight-grained heart pine, were used to keep the walls and ceilings level and straight. Using the tapered seven-foot straight edge and the four-foot Darbies, properly was an art form because the finish coat would exactly reflect the shape of the brown-coated wall. If the brown coat was crooked or lumped up, the finish white coat would also be crooked and lumped up.

The finish application began in the corners of the ceiling and then the ceiling itself. Then we finished the top portions of the walls down about four feet to where the brown coat was joined. The scaffold was moved and the bottom portion of the wall was scraped with the trowels to knock down any high points.

Sometimes, the final white coat was a sand finish using clean white sand. Where it started drying, it was rubbed with a rubber float and light water sprinkle if needed to bring the white sand to the top. When a hard coat was desired, no sand was used, and the plaster had to be troweled quite a bit until you heard the singing steel trowels and you could almost see your reflection in the hard finish.

During the finish coat, a high quality paintbrush was used to sprinkle water on the wall or ceiling, so that the trowel could blend in any imperfections of the finish coat. This system of completing the brown coat from the bottom and the white coat from the top was used to prevent any kind of visible joint between the brown coat and the white coat.

That February day, I recall looking out the window at the battered lime box sitting in the side yard for nearly a week and seeing bags of dry, powdered lime that would be placed in water in preparation for the screening process. Screening plaster is a dirty job, but a very important one.

C.W. Major dipped out buckets of the lime and placed it on a screen. He used a tee-shaped wooden paddle to push the lime through the screen so no hard pieces or foreign material would be in the mixture when it was brought into the house. If there were any hard pieces in the plaster, they would create a small trench when troweled. The only way to fix the trench would be to find the hard piece and remove it—then, put a small amount of plaster on the trowel and swipe the area again.

After the screened plaster was ready, it was poured on the large plaster board about the size of a half sheet of plywood so that all four plasterers could help with the mixing. We formed a space in the middle of the soft lime on the mortar board with our trowel so water could be poured in and the hardening agent could be sprinkled into the clean water. When the mixing process was complete we had white coat plaster. We didn't have much time before it started to harden, so we troweled it on the ceiling and walls carefully and in a hurry.

On that particular day, Uncle Charlie Pacetti told me, "Pee in the can and use it as part of the mixing water. The urine will act as an agent to slow down the hardening process and give us a little more time to work the plaster on the walls." As the youngest plasterer on the scaffold, I did what I was told and peed in the can, using it to mix the batch. Whether or not this was true, I don't know, but when we mixed urine into the plaster, there was no discoloration or odor.

At this point, all four of us used our trowels to mix the large batch of snow white plaster with the grayish hardener and light yellow pee, until it was fully blended and white as snow. When this process was accomplished, we knew we had limited time to get the plaster on the wall before it hardened. We filled our hawk and picked a corner of the room to work. Two men worked together to put the plaster in the corners where the ceilings met the walls. This was a critical part because crooked lines are quickly spotted. There would be no crooked lines or walls with our crew! It was a great experience.

Plastering has become a lost art because installing sheet rock is cheaper and faster, but for those of us who

MINORCAN GUMBO FOR THE SOUL

were taught the old ways, plastering will always be a special expertise that was fun and instantly gratifying.

I look back on my days in the trade as some of the happiest times of my life. I still see places in St. Augustine where I worked. There are many buildings still standing where I might have laid a few bricks or poured concrete or plastered.

Building something is rewarding and many aspects of it will never change. When I was on the scaffold or digging footers for a building, I knew I had to get it done, and there wasn't much time for jabber. I could not be lazy and successful in the masonry trade. It's still that way.

This is the hawk and trowel I purchased in 1956 when I became an apprentice bricklayer, plasterer, and cement finisher in St. Augustine, Florida. I don't remember the make of the hawk, but the trowel is a Marshalltown. I still have these two tools, and I sometimes take them out of the drawer and hold them. The last time I used them was in the late 1990s when I stuccoed a concrete retaining wall for Ted Steinmeyer at his mother's lake house. I thought my left arm would fall off from holding up that stucco on the hawk for about four straight hours. No telling what it would feel like now considering how out of shape my plastering muscles have become. Nevertheless, I thoroughly enjoyed my years in the mortar box.

A Saturday in Remembrance of My Mother

FOUR OR FIVE cars loaded with family members arrived at the northern quadrant of San Lorenzo Cemetery in St. Augustine, Florida, around 9:30 a.m. on Saturday, February 16, 2002, to offer final respects to Mary Frances Brinson "Nanny" Jones.

Richard, Angie, Ricky, Susan, Lessie, John, Stewart, Shaun, Aunt Pat, Kay, Bill, Stephanie, Scott, Lee, Mark, Luke, Mike, Carol, Scott, Cindy, Mindy, and Bobby were all there hugging – happy and loving on each other.

The Craig Funeral Home's bright blue canopy was easy to spot among the wind-gnarled oak trees. There were green covered chairs and a green rug near the site where Nanny's ashes were soon to be buried. Nanny's marker would be in place in about six weeks.

Her grave adjoins many St. Augustine folks, including the Critchlows, who were Nanny's landlord when

A SATURDAY IN REMEMBRANCE OF MY MOTHER

she lived on St. George Street in the 1960s. Malinda and I lived down the street from the Critchlow's at 312 St. George in the old Redmond House where our third child, second daughter Laurie was born.

At 9:50 a.m., a very dark-skinned priest from India arrived and introduced himself to the family. He recognized that we were a big, happy family and that Mary must have been proud of us. "She was," I told him. Father then performed a very short but meaningful service. At the conclusion, we bowed our heads and prayed for the happy repose of Nanny's soul. This fine priest from India made Nanny's service complete because this proud daughter of Dixie had a northern lady do the readings at church. Then she had an Indian priest perform the last services. Was the Holy Ghost in charge or what?

After the service we drove through town on Ponce de Leon Boulevard and picked up A1A on May Street. We drove to Mayport to spread Nanny's memorial service roses on the St. Johns River.

"Meet at the parking lot of the Le Cruz gambling ship, and go on the dock," I told everyone. Unfortunately, the Le Cruz directions I gave were wrong because the ship was about a mile north of where I meant. However, everybody figured out I had given the wrong address. Thank God, Mayport only has one street adjacent to the river and, no traffic lights, so we all finally gathered at the correct parking lot before noon.

MINORCAN GUMBO FOR THE SOUL

The sky was cobalt blue after the morning fog lifted. There was a soft west wind blowing easy across the river right in our faces and the temperature was pleasant for a mid-winter day in February. Next to the dock where we were standing, a Mayport shrimp boat was tied to the pilings of the adjoining dock. The name of the shrimp boat was *Captain Richard*. Was the Holy Spirit at work here or what?

When everyone was together on the dock, each of us took a handful of dried roses that Susan had prepared and after a moment of personal reflection we tossed the flowers into the river in memory of Nanny. Anyone who knew Nanny knew she did not like deep water and especially didn't like deep water where sharks might be present. When we tossed Nanny's rose petals into the river, they didn't float out to sea. They took advantage of the tide and west wind and floated right back to the shore. There was no way those flowers were leaving Mayport. Again, was the Holy Spirit at work here or what?

After a few more tears and strong hugs, the group meandered two blocks north to Bill and Angie's restaurant to do what the Jones family always does when it is in crisis or happy or sad or whatever – eat ... and usually eat something fried.

The platters of seafood were scrumptious, and the service, though slow, was polite and accommodating. Whatever we wanted, we got. The owner even set up a

A SATURDAY IN REMEMBRANCE OF MY MOTHER

VCR with Disney tapes for young Mark, Luke, and Judy, who were sitting there with pent-up energy.

We sat down for lunch at 12:45 p.m. and finished at 3:00 p.m. We had a joyful visit with each other. It was a great day with a group of great people. Nanny would have been proud. May her soul, and the souls of all the faithfully departed, through the mercy of God Rest in Peace. Amen.

Richard Jones-Cousin Kay Manning-Malinda Jones

Fishing with Grandson Mike Jones

ON MAY 15, 2004, Mike stayed up until 1:30 a.m. in Whigham, Georgia watching a movie with his sister, Melanie, and the family. He left the house at 6:15 a.m. to drive to Tallahassee to go fishing with his Gampa. He arrived at my home on Pink Flamingo Drive at 8:00 a.m.

It was a beautiful day with few clouds in the sky and no prediction of rain or strong winds. By 8:30 a.m. we had left for mostly unchartered waters.

We arrived at Crawfordville Storage Company around 9:00 a.m. to pick up my 1976, 19-foot Mako center console that was stored on a grassy field adjoining the storage sheds. Before hooking up the boat, I opened my 4x6-foot rented storage shed and retrieved two coolers for our food. We planned a light lunch of fried chicken, fried chicken, fried chicken, Vienna sausages for dessert, Goldfish cheese crackers, and lots of Diet Cokes and

FISHING WITH GRANDSON MIKE JONES

Dr. Peppers. We planned a picnic on the porch of Big 10 Hunting Camp far up the Apalachicola River near Howard Creek. We didn't plan to run out of food in the event of motor failure or anything unforeseen.

We removed the canvas cover from the boat, put the coolers into the boat, hooked up all the lights and safety chains on the trailer hitch, and proceeded to drive out of the yard headed to Apalachicola.

When I put the Dodge pickup truck in gear and started forward, however, we heard a loud clunk. Still, we thought nothing of it. I pulled the boat along the sand driveway out to US 98 and quickly pulled out on the highway. Then, we heard a loud screech and I looked in the rearview mirror. Smoke was coming from the right side of the trailer. I pulled off the road on the shoulder and told Mike one of the wheels must be frozen and unable to roll.

Mike got out of the car. When I joined him, I asked, "What's the matter?"

"Gampa, you forgot to take the chain off the wheel you wrapped around the fender to keep anyone from stealing the boat," he said with a grin.

He was tickled, and I was sad that I had stepped in it. Sure enough, there was the Master padlock and heavy chain wound so tightly that it bent the aluminum fender.

I looked at Mike and said, "You are never too old to step in some dumbass."

He agreed with a belly laugh and a big smile that

lasted a long time.

I always carry a pair of bolt cutters in the toolbox because you never know when things like this will happen. I cut the chain in three places so that it would release its death grip from the fender, which it did with a loud bang. Mike then knelt in the sand and untangled the chain that was tightly wrapped around the axle. I slung the old chain and lock in the bed of the truck with a vengeance and started out once again for Apalachicola with my vessel in tow.

Things were pretty uneventful for the rest of the trip to and from Big 10. The wind was blowing pretty hard, but we were able to run about thirty miles per hour when we got into the main part of the river all the way to the dock at Big 10.

We took two white plastic chairs from the screened porch and sat them on the dock. We proceeded to eat chicken and think about all the good times we had at this special place in past years. We talked about Gene Raffield and how we felt his spirit all around the camp. The oyster shucking table was still there, as were all the trees that held tons of buckshot from target practice. We talked about Chris Doolin, and we figured he and the young ones must have shot at least 5,000 rounds of 22 caliber bullets across the river with his automatic rifle. How many young boys shot their first gun at this special place?

The ride on the Apalachicola River is always beautiful.

FISHING WITH GRANDSON MIKE JONES

The water was normal stage, so there was plenty of high ground to walk on. Trees were myriad shades of green, and the moss looked like ballet dancers with such graceful moves to and fro in the wind.

The only downside of the trip was seeing the influx of house boats up and down the river. One of the new houseboats was within fifty feet of the Big 10 dock. The nearness of the new houseboat made target practice to the south of the camp a thing of the past. People can unintentionally ruin a fine place full of memories but the newbies were not breaking any laws and had the same right to be there as us.

We got back to the boat ramp under the Apalachicola Bridge and drove the boat onto the trailer with no problems whatsoever. We then decided we needed a big bowl of oyster stew at Boss Oyster's, so away we went.

When I parked the truck across the street from Boss Oyster, Mike looked at the tire which had been chained and saw that it was flat. The trailer had two wheels and tires on both sides, so we weren't stuck at this spot. We walked over to it and saw a nice big hole that came from dragging it across US 98 for several hundred feet.

We said "to heck with it" and decided to handle it after we slurped up our stew. The oyster stew at Boss Oyster's is as good as any we ever tasted. Afterward, I drove to the local BP station on one good tire on one side of the trailer. The owner called Ace Hardware and learned they had a lug wrench for sale that would get the wheel off. I pulled to the back of the station, unhooked the boat, and had Mike sit there as I searched for and found the Ace place.

We got the wrench. I broke the rusty nuts loose by practically standing on the lug wrench. Mike took the flat tire off and put on the new tire. We hooked up the boat and made it back to the storage place and home without further incident.

When we arrived home around 5:00 p.m., I immediately fell asleep in my chair. A little later on, Mike grilled steaks for us, and we watched *Valdez Is Comin*, starring Burt Lancaster, one of my favorite movies. All in all, it was a very good day.

The Fishing Trip from Hell

THE 2006 ANNUAL Southeastern Fisheries Association convention was over, and five of us looked forward to fishing in the deep waters offshore Key Largo. I had been to the emergency center in Islamorada the previous night to get an antibiotic shot in my butt to cure a case of cellulitis in my left leg. I felt triumphant to still be going on the fishing trip. We knew we could catch some big grouper if we could hire a charter boat operated by a professional. All of us had caught many, many fish in our collective lifetimes.

The early morning sky was dark gray, and the palm fronds in front of the Key Largo Motel swayed gently from the easterly breeze. Everything was wet from the morning rain, and the sweet smell of flowers filled the air.

I woke up about 5:30 a.m. and had coffee with Mindy. Then I walked downstairs to get the car and pick up my son, Matt, Eugene, and Randy Raffield so we could meet Tom Hill in front of the motel. Squeezing four bulky bodies into a small SRX was the first indication maybe we should all go back to our rooms and order room service.

But no way! We stopped at a Circle K gas station on the way to Key Largo Fisheries to buy some breakfast and coffee, during which we were confronted with attitude beyond belief. It must have been time for a change in shifts, and the woman taking orders and making change sneered at us and didn't seem to care whether we liked the cheese biscuit or not. We shook our heads and smiled, knowing that bad attitudes are nationwide.

We missed this hint that it wasn't the best day for our trip. We had already had two signs before we had gone a mile.

"The charter boat itself is a little rough, but the captain has a reputation for catching big grouper," Tom Hill said.

That was good enough for us. After all, we didn't need an air conditioned Hatteras to catch fish. We just needed a solid platform, proper bait and a professional captain and crew to put us near the fish.

When we reached the parking lot at Key Largo Fisheries and walked toward the dock where the boats were tied up, we all had a strange feeling. The charter boat we spotted was less than adequately maintained and we were concerned by how top heavy it looked. But the Raffield brothers know a top heavy boat when they see one and they did not say anything. The captain had been

THE FISHING TRIP FROM HELL

a commercial fisherman who converted the boat to recreational charter boat fishing.

"Where are the life vests?" we asked.

No response but we assumed they were in a locker somewhere,

The captain was a large man not in the best of health. In fact, it was difficult for him to move. The young crewman looked twice as rough.

"Would it be all right if my girlfriend goes fishing with us?" he asked.

"I drove up to Fort Lauderdale to pick her up at one a.m., and we haven't slept yet."

He might have been telling the truth, but the couch, which really was a house couch, looked like it had been slept in by all kinds of people and pets and had not had the sheet or cover changed since the late 1990s.

We looked at each other and glanced at Matt, who was treating us to the trip. Matt is a gentleman, so he nodded "yes."

Here we were, about to go offshore with a relatively young woman on board, which gave us a trio of charter fishing folks who fit the category of "rode hard and put up wet."

"Do we get to keep the fish?" we asked the captain.

"We're from North Florida and won't pay for a charter if we have to give the captain any of the fish so he can sell them."

"I always let the customers keep all the fish if they want them," he said. We had brought our trusty Styrofoam coolers to take the fish back with us.

After all of that had been taken care of, we got on the boat. (I can't remember the name of the boat.) But before we could shove off, the captain said, "I need to get ice, gas, and bait."

"Hello!" I whispered to Matt, "Didn't he know we were coming?"

The captain managed to get the single diesel engine started, put it in gear, and pull from his slip over to the Key Largo Fisheries fuel pumps where we helped fill the tanks. Tom brought out shovels full of ice and all kinds of bait. We helped stow everything and clean up the mess. We were working our butts off on a paid charter trip.

The hand-carved wooden plug for one of the built-in ice chests was missing, so there was a small confrontation between the captain and his crewman about its loss. We collectively rolled our eyes and started having second thoughts.

The voyage of the Minnow came to mind because the captain looked straight out of "Gilligan's Island," and the crewman could have passed for a hyped-up Gilligan. His girlfriend would not have been mistaken for Ginger or Maryann.

We finally left the dock after more than an hour from the time we arrived and headed out the narrow channel to the Atlantic Ocean. That's when Randy, the crewman, said, "The wind will start to pick up and get stronger as the day goes by."

This was the third indication to turn back, but we were fired up just thinking about bringing back a box of big black grouper or bull dolphins. A fisherman's mind is a scary place, and you should never go there alone! Mindy and I had just read about not venturing into the deep recesses of your mind without taking a friend along. Very scary.

As the "vessel" idled down the channel past all kinds of boats and houses, we commented on how much work it must have been to blast through all the coral to open up this channel. This whole area had been a natural reef until population growth and development began many decades earlier.

Eugene and Randy Raffield were scoping out the situation, checking the electronics and fishing gear. I think they even listened to the hum of the engine to see if it was running on all cylinders like it should. We cut the fool and made small talk as we reached the end of the channel, and the captain pushed the throttle forward. We seemed to quickly get up on a plane. The seas near shore were less than three feet, but you could see the massive buffaloes running offshore in front of the northeast wind.

The greenish water was muddy, but still pretty. It was easy to tell when you got into the blue water at the deeper depths. We ran north and east for about 45 minutes. The boat was comfortable enough once it quartered the waves.

We saw a few other boats headed offshore, including a couple of 23-foot center consoles. So, I thought we would be fine.

Once we reached a particular spot, the captain dropped the anchor and we started chumming for live bait. We were after live ballyhoo, but there was also another type of baitfish we wanted because the captain said each one of those would catch a black grouper. I could feel my greedy glands kick into gear just thinking about the possibility of bringing in a 35-pound black grouper.

We were catching live ballyhoo with small poles, and when I tried to get the hook out, it caught my left hand and became imbedded a little bit. I took some pliers and pulled it out because the barb wasn't very far into my skin.

"You might need some alcohol on that to prevent infection," Tom said.

"Don't worry about Pops," Matt said. "He has enough antibiotics in him right now to undergo an operation."

We seemed to stay in the baitfishing mode far longer than any of us thought necessary. Once the captain pulled out a square net, and the Raffield boys figured out what he was trying to do, they took over the baitfish routine. They could have loaded the boat within a few minutes.

"The Raffield family has probably harvested fifty million pounds of baitfish over the life of the company," I told the captain and mate. I think the fifty million-pound figure caused their eyes to glaze over, and I don't think they believed it. But that figure was conservative.

We finally had all of the live bait the captain wanted, so he proceeded to take us to his honey hole.

The wind had picked up considerably. When the waves slammed the boat on either side, it was difficult to stand because the boat rocked like a bell buoy in a summer squall. This is when I said the name of the boat should be, "Rock and Roll."

There were quite a few boats near the honey hole, all in a line running from southeast to northwest. So, I figured there must be a ridge or coral reef running in that particular area.

We anchored in line with the other boats, and the mate put several big poles over. It looked to me like they had a ten-foot wire leader and about two pounds of weight. I wondered how we would ever feed the fish and how hard it was going to be to wind in a big fish and lots of lead weight. That turned out to not be a problem.

We may have had a bite, but I can't remember. We were all looking at a series of black clouds headed our way and wondering if it was the beginning of the high winds that were predicted for the following day. The rain started soon and came in vertical sheets instead of a straight downpour.

The captain was aloft, sitting in the only chair up

there and getting pretty wet, but just put on his yellow slicker. We stayed dry if we pushed way into the open cabin. Nobody wanted to go into the forward cabin because we didn't know what kind of creatures or critters were living in that dark, dank place.

After a while, we told the captain we had had enough and wanted to go back to the dock. He raised the anchor, and we started back. The mate thought we might try to troll on the way back, so he put a big rod with a 20-foot wire leader and a large piece of bait into the rod holder and set the pressure for the drag.

"If a fish gets on, just leave the rod in the holder and reel in the fish while it's there," he said. I looked at him like he was nuts. Why in the world would someone want to catch a fish by using the rod holder and not put the butt of the pole on your belt buckle to reel in your fish?

"Maybe they're afraid some pilgrim will drop the pole overboard if it's taken out of the rod holder," I thought. We had no interest in catching a fish that way, so we told him to forget it. "Let's get back to shore."

The captain was up in the tuna tower and couldn't hear us, but soon, we heard the motor go silent. The mate scurried to open up a hatch and do something I could not see. When he finished, he said something about a leak in the area and if it hadn't been fixed, we would have been in trouble. I was a little relieved when the captain started the engine.

THE FISHING TRIP FROM HELL

For some reason, though, the captain didn't head into the strong winds or even quarter the sea. He stayed in between so that each wave slammed into our port side, rocking the boat fiercely. Randy punched Eugene in the side and said, "Take a look at the mate's girlfriend." She was wearing a life vest, and we wondered what was going on because we were not told to put on life vests.

I was worried and working on a plan in my mind, in the event that the boat sunk. I looked for some rope so that we could tie ourselves together in the water until someone came to pull us out. I really had doubts as to how many more slams the boat could take. The waves were a good seven feet or bigger. Nobody was seasick, however, because fear triumphs over weak stomachs.

Matt knew I was worried, and like all of my children, he wanted to make sure "the old man" was okay and would be okay no matter what happened to the boat.

Another wave slammed the port side of the boat, and everyone except Tom Hill uttered an expletive. It was at this point that Matt practically jumped up to the top of the ladder where the captain could hear every word he said and shouted, "Get this *#@%*# boat back to shore, and get the bow into the waves. And do it now!" The boat immediately started quartering the waves, and we didn't get hit with any more sidewise waves for the rest of the trip.

If I had been the captain and seen the look on Matt's face, I guarantee I would have done what Matt told me to do just as quickly or quicker than that captain did.

We reached the smoother bay waters in about forty-five minutes. We all heaved a great sigh of relief; although the mate's girlfriend didn't take her life vest off until the boat was tied at the dock.

We were more than happy to get off that boat. Matt paid the captain, and without saying a word, we left to go back to our families a little bit wiser and a little bit older. We will never make the mistake again to go offshore without knowing more about the boat and the captain.

Epilogue

We visited Key Largo Fisheries where Tom, Dottie, and Rick provided us with a "goodie box" of fresh grouper for our supper. The next morning, Mindy and I left the motel at 5:00 a.m. We didn't get out of driving winds and rain until we reached Homestead. I haven't been offshore on a Keys charter boat since.

My Uncle Lester

Staff Sergeant Philip Lester Brinson, Army Air Corps
Killed In Action--September 9, 1943
Service # 34208695 – Tail Gunner B-26
322nd Bombardment Group 450th Bomb Squadron
Air Offensive Europe Campaign
Motto: "I fear none in doing right."

UNCLE PHILIP LESTER Brinson was born in East Mayport, Florida, on November 16, 1917. His niece, my dear sister, Lesta Ann Sasser, was named in his honor. Uncle Lester was the son of Patrick Philip Brinson and Mary Eliza Lester Brinson. He had two older sisters, Mary Frances Brinson Jones (Nanny) and Julia Patricia Brinson Shugart (Aunt Pat), who became a GOLD STAR FAMILY when Uncle Lester was killed in action.

Uncle Lester's family moved to Key West in the late 1920s. His name is listed in the 1930 Federal Census as living in Key West with his father, stepmother, and two sisters. The Brinson family next moved to Miami and lived next door to the Willie and Bernice Carey family who lived at 857 NW 21st Terrace. Uncle Lester moved to St. Augustine as a teenager, lived in Miami after that for awhile.

Captain Willie Carey was a commercial lobster and conch fisherman in Biscayne Bay. Unfortunately, there are no pictures of Uncle Lester during his early years in Key West.

Uncle Lester was inducted at Camp Blanding, Florida, on July 3, 1942. At the time of his enlistment, the records show that he was 5'9", weighed 135 pounds, and was a glazier by profession. He was the perfect size to serve as a tail gunner in a B-26.

The *St. Augustine Record* quoted Uncle Lester in its July 9, 1942, edition of the paper. The reporter wrote about the attitude of the new enlisted men and the article said in part, "These men have very definite ideas as to what they are fighting for and the task they have ahead of them. Regardless of what they did in civil life, their education, or their background, all are determined to protect their national heritage of freedom in a democracy. The war to Philip Lester Brinson, 24, of No. 146 Cunningham Avenue, a glazier, is, "not a war of today but is one which will determine how future generations will live."

What beautiful and profound words from a young man who would be killed in action before he reached his

MY UNCLE LESTER

26th birthday. For everyone related to Uncle Lester, remember these words to fully appreciate and understand that he knew what road he had to travel and, knowing this, was willing to put his life on the line for all of us. That kind of attitude and resolve is what turns regular people into heroes.

Uncle Lester was nicknamed "Boy." I asked Nanny why he was given that nickname and she gave me that certain look only Nanny could give and said, "Because he was the only boy in the family." Duh! I felt a little dumb but thought the answer might have been more revealing than a statement of the obvious.

"Boy" was deeply loved by Nanny and Aunt Pat. The few times he came to our house at 146 Cunningham Drive in St. Augustine I knew he was special. He was trained at Camp Blanding and Barksdale Air Base, Louisiana and made it to St. Augustine on weekend passes several times.

He was being trained as a tail gunner for the B-26 Martin Marauder. The Marauder was a rugged, sturdy airplane. It took a lot of time for new pilots to fully understand and control the two Pratt & Whitney 2800 Radial Engines. The power and torque of the massive engines and the shorter wingspan in the early models made it a challenge to fly even for experienced instructors. There were over 5,000 Marauders built for WWII. At one time the B-26 had two tails but was changed to one in order to give tail gunners like Uncle Lester a better view of enemy aircraft during bombing missions.

He was almost killed at Barksdale Air Base during the gunner training phase of his service when his plane crashed on the base runway. Everyone but Uncle Lester and one of his buddies died in the crash. I read a news account of it once, but I can't find the clipping anymore.

What a trauma it must have been to crash, see your buddies die, and then clean up, strap it back on, and climb into the rear turret of another plane for more training. What a challenge for a 24-year-old, peace-loving man. The Greatest Generation for sure.

That wasn't his time to die. He was given leave for a few days after the crash to come to St. Augustine and catch his breath. These were tough young men--a special breed.

I haven't been able to get the actual record of Uncle Lester's last mission yet, so what follows is information from many stories I have read about the 322nd and other bombardment groups.

I sent several requests asking for help to find information about him. I received a prompt response from a man in Norway who has studied B-26 Marauders as his hobby for the last eight years. He sent emails with specific information. He thought he may know of the airplane Uncle Lester was on the day he was killed. Alf Johannsen sent this, and I thank him for his concern and help:

Plane #118058 Bomb Group 450, Bomb Squadron

MY UNCLE LESTER

322, Pilots name was Lt. Jerome B. Reynolds; Last action was shot down by flak over target. Date shot down 09 09 43. This is an official Air Force record, and it seems to me this was the B-26 Uncle Lester was fighting from when he died.

Uncle Lester was killed in action before the 322nd participated in the Battle of the Bulge in December 1944-January 1945. I learned about the 322nd being in the Battle of the Bulge while doing this research. It is very nostalgic, as I knew and worked with two soldiers who fought in the Battle of the Bulge, Charlie Lyles and Ernie Premetz, both of whom were in my fish world.

There was Charlie Lyles from Mississippi, who worked for the Bureau of Commercial Fisheries and the Gulf States Marine Fisheries Commission, and there was Ernie Premetz, who was the executive director of the South Atlantic Fishery Management Council. These were two good men from the Greatest Generation.

Following are some statistics on the 8th Air Force I retrieved from the Internet. Uncle Lester was serving in the 8th when he was killed.

"The 8th Air Force became the greatest air armada used by any country in any war, reaching a total strength of 200,000 personnel by mid-1944. It could put, over a single target, more than 2000 four engine heavy bombers and 1000 fighters. For this reason the 8th Air force became known as the 'Mighty 8th.'

MINORCAN GUMBO FOR THE SOUL

Half of the USAAF casualties during World War II were suffered by the 8th Air Force during its strategic bombing campaign over Europe.

Over 26,000 young airmen were killed in action (one tenth of all Americans killed in WWII), 18,000 wounded and 28,000 taken prisoner during the daylight raids over Germany. Despite these tremendous losses, the 'Mighty 8th' was never turned back from a mission because of enemy action.

Airmen of the 8th Air Force were awarded 17 Congressional Medals of Honor, 220 Distinguished Service Crosses, 850 Silver Stars, 7,000 Purple Hearts, 46,000 Distinguished Flying Crosses and 442,000 Air Medals."

One of the reasons I wrote this story about Uncle Lester is to give closure for Aunt Pat, Lessie, and myself as the immediate family because Uncle Lester's body was never found. I had a chance to know him, as did my late brother Richard, but Lessie was born seventeen days after he was killed.

I want my children, grandchildren, and great grandchildren to know and be grateful and proud that my Uncle Lester, along with 26,000 other young men who were in the Army Air Force, died for our country. I know schoolchildren are taught a very little bit about World War II, but I hope our family's descendants are aware of the direct involvement of an ancestor who gave his life for their

MY UNCLE LESTER

freedom. When you hear the words "patriot" or "warrior" or "defender," think about Uncle Lester, and say a little prayer for him and for yourself.

Mary Frances Jones with her brother SSgt Philip Lester Brinson KIA

A Name on a Monument in St. Augustine

I WAS EIGHT years old, living at 146 Cunningham Drive, when America entered World War II on December 7, 1941. Walking downtown to the plaza from North City was a normal family occurrence. The plaza was the gathering place for soldiers going through basic training in Camp Blanding and Coast Guardsmen stationed at the historic Ponce de Leon Hotel.

I loved listening to the live music performed in the Band Shell by military bands. I especially loved patriotic songs. I was always proud of soldiers marching on the fort green and along Bay Street in perfect step.

Veronica Lake, one of the most popular Hollywood stars in the 1940s, came to St. Augustine to help sell war bonds. She, Paulette Goddard, and Dorothy Lamour were known as the "Sweater, the Sarong and the Peek-a-boo Bang."

A NAME ON A MONUMENT IN ST. AUGUSTINE

Veronica Lake stood on a flatbed trailer in front of the Matanzas Theatre, urging the noisy crowd to buy war bonds. I remember the words and melody of Irving Berlin's song: "Any bonds today? Bonds of freedom, that's what I'm selling, any bonds today? Scrape up the most you can, here comes the freedom man asking you to buy a share of freedom today." Strange how some songs linger with you all your life.

I lived that wartime memory again on November 4, 2013. My wife, Malinda, and I were walking down King Street along the plaza sidewalk toward the Bridge of Lions. We stopped for a minute at the east entrance of the Old Market Place then continued to the northeast corner. The World War II monument we came to visit was mostly blocked by large electrical boxes. We were upset with the disrespect for those who died in WWI, WWII, Korea and Vietnam.

On the monument's large bronze plaque are 72 names of St. Augustine heroes killed in World War II. My uncle, SSgt. Philip Lester Brinson, is the fifth name on the first row.

The WWII Monument before and after. Oorah!

November 4, 2013   *May 25, 2014*

I touched the bronze plaque on the monument and gently rubbed Uncle Lester's name with my fingers like I have been doing for decades each time I am uptown in St. Augustine. I anticipated a lump in my throat and tears in my eyes. The lump came first followed by a few tears. I will always be proud of my Uncle Lester who gave it all.

Mindy and I stepped back from the monument to the sidewalk. I became a little angry that the only marker in the world listing the St. Augustine men who gave their lives was dishonored by the placement of Department of Transportation electrical boxes. The boxes should not block the view of the monument.

When we returned to Tallahassee, I decided something had to be done about all the equipment blocking the monument. I wrote Lynne Stephenson, President-elect of the St. Augustine Pilot Club. The Pilot Club was responsible for establishing the beautiful monument in the first place. I explained who I was, in regard to my uncle's name being on the monument and giving his life in WWII. I asked if they could set up a fund to relocate the electrical boxes blocking the monument, and if the electrical boxes could not be moved, then they could relocate the monument to a more appropriate location on the plaza grounds.

The Pilot Club responded immediately and was very interested in fixing the monument's location. They wrote the city mayor asking for removal of the boxes. His response was less than anticipated and centered on the cost of moving the electrical boxes. I drove back to St. Augustine for an interview with a reporter for the *St. Augustine Record* a few weeks later. I gave him my background and why I was interested in cleaning up the site of the monument that honored all those who died for America.

At the same time I contacted one of my dearest friends, Master Chief Bill Lee - Seal Team 10 - who recently retired after thirty years in the Navy. Master Chief Lee contacted the VFW in St. Augustine. Shortly afterwards Mr. Glenn Tilley wrote a strongly worded 'guest opinion' on behalf of the VFW. He advocated very strongly that the WWII monument deserved to be honored and the VFW fully supported all efforts to do so.

Everyone in St. Augustine who learned about this project was energized and enthused. It was a 'no-brainer.' Many people played a part in "doing the right thing for the right reason," as they teach in the USMC. The entire

MINORCAN GUMBO FOR THE SOUL

community stepped up, so I knew something good was going to happen.

The *St. Augustine Record* played a huge role in bringing the citizens together. I spent time doing what I could. Maybe my best contribution was simply pointing out the fact that the monument was no longer in a place of honor. The citizens made sure it was fixed. Now we have a very wonderful area honoring all the St. Augustine heroes who died for our nation. Oorah!

Bob & Mindy Jones & Lessie Jones Sasser

War Monument rededicated May 26, 2014

I received this letter from a fellow veteran from a family of patriots. I accept his heartfelt thanks on behalf of all those who helped restore our monument.

Good morning, Mr. Jones.

>*I just wanted to thank you for being such a thoughtful and concerned veteran in your seeing to it that the Vietnam Memorial in the park, downtown St. Augustine, was moved to a more*

A NAME ON A MONUMENT IN ST. AUGUSTINE

respectful location. My father, SSG John A. Thiele, Jr., died in Vietnam and his name is on that memorial. I am a retired 25-year veteran, my stepfather (COL William T. Carcaba) is a 34-year veteran, my stepbrother (MSG William T. Carcaba - Tony) a 32-year veteran, my uncle (John Carcaba) is a retired Naval Aviator, and my grandfather (John A. Thiele, Sr.) was a 100% disabled instructor pilot in the Army Air Corps. The military has been a way of life for me since birth and I remember many things about my father (fortunately) although I was just shy of five years old whenever we were given the news of his death by a death notification officer whenever we lived at 21 Old Mission Avenue. Words cannot begin to convey my deep appreciation for your generosity and patriotic actions. You are a shining example of a kind and caring soul. Thank you for giving me hope in this incredibly selfish society that we live in. I think it is neat that we are both natives of St. Augustine and that you live in Tallahassee, FL. I was stationed over in Tallahassee from 1999 to 2001 and I am an avid Florida State Seminole fan. My stepbrother, Steven Carcaba, is the owner of St. Augustine Precast & Stone here in St. Augustine. He did work on the Korean War Memorial there in Tallahassee and I am so proud of him. I think it is a safe bet that we have a lot in common and that you will always be in my prayers. God Bless you, Mr. Jones, and I wish you and your family the best that life has to offer.

Kind regards,

MSG (Ret) Christopher A. Thiele

"I Think They Will"

I HOPPED OUT of bed at 5:00 a.m. for the round-trip drive to Mississippi and back to certify two young men at Clark Seafood Company, a very old seafood company and former member of Southeastern Fisheries Association.

Miss Mindy, the weather maven I have slept with the past sixty-three years was already up. As I walked into the kitchen, she flipped open her I-Pad and checked the weather between Tallahassee and Pascagoula, Mississippi.

"Hey, Big Boy," she said using her index finger and thumb to maximize the picture of the weather cells on the screen. "You are going to be in heavy rain from here to Marianna and then again when you get to Chipley."

"Ain't no hill for a climber," I said to her for the umpteenth time since 1950. "I'll be careful."

She blew me a kiss and smiled.

Mindy was right. The weather when I pulled out the driveway at 6:00 a.m. was horrible. It stopped for a little while near Marianna then came back with a vengeance when I got to Chipley, just like Mindy predicted. It did not stop completely until I reached the Pensacola Bridge and glanced at a small rainbow over Scenic Drive. My 2010 Yukon is a great vehicle because I can put it in all-wheel drive on the fly and immediately feel more traction, especially on slick roads.

The 530-mile round trip drive to perform food safety chores was uneventful even though the roads were bumper to bumper in Mobile on my way back to Tallahassee. The Senator Bankhead Tunnel was stop and go. When the traffic completely stopped inside the tunnel there was a cacophony of horn blowing that first timers often like to do. After making it through the tunnel, the rest of the drive was okay. I got home at 6:00 p.m., still in heavy rain in Tallahassee, just another routine 12-hour day at the office...except for one thing.

I ate my usual two eggs and grits around 5:30 a.m. After fighting the traffic since then I was a little hungry by 10:00 a.m. As luck, or a Higher Power would have it, a large highway sign indicated a Cracker Barrel was at the next exit about a mile away. I got off and parked as far away as I could so I could make Mindy happy and get my morning walk in. I approached the lady in charge of seating and saw the second room was empty. I asked for the table way back in the corner by the window, which she obliged. I planned to catch up on my e-mail and make any necessary telephone calls because Mindy made me

"I THINK THEY WILL"

promise to keep both my hands on the steering wheel in bad weather.

When my toast and coffee came, I noticed two elderly ladies on walkers striding with great fervor into the room and take a seat at the table next to me. The waitresses added three more tables to accommodate the three wheel chairs being rolled into the room. Then several more elderly seniors were brought in and seated by the two attendants. Not a word was spoken.

I thought for a moment as my reverie was broken, why did they have to be seated right next to me when all I wanted was a little quiet time. Then I looked at the scene again, realizing that could be me or Mindy sitting at that table. It was at that precise moment I looked intensely at them, one at a time. I made eye contact with the man, but he glanced away. There was a lady with brown, curly hair that looked like she had just come from a beauty parlor. All the others were warmly dressed and neat as can be. There weren't many smiles. That made me sad.

Directly across from me was a smallish lady with snow white hair who had the most astonishingly colored blue eyes I have ever seen.

They were neither dark nor light blue, but almost a faded Carolina Blue. She wore a white long sleeve sweater around her frail shoulders. Her facial wrinkles were drawn in beautiful artistic lines, almost as if they were sketched in place each morning. I could not take my eyes off the wrinkles around her mouth that pointed up like she had been happy all her life. We made eye contact and smiled. I immediately thought of my mother and Mindy's mother and almost lost it right there sitting alone at my corner table in a Cracker Barrel restaurant in Spanish Fort, Alabama.

The name on the badge of the young waitress serving them was Makallah. I concentrated on the manner in which she was performing her job for a few minutes. She must have come from a loving home. She was comfortable among these eight seniors. She was pleasant and patient with them, smiling and talking in a soothing voice to each patron. I was stirred with a strong emotions, watching her take each breakfast order. I realized I was not in charge and that God has a plan for me and today He was offering me a loving glimpse of the future. If we are lucky we will all get old and frail.

I finished my coffee and asked Makallah to walk with me for a minute. I think she knew what I wanted because she offered a sweet smile. When we left the area where the elders were sitting I said, "I want to buy breakfast for that table without them knowing it. What do I need to do?" She was moved by my request to pay it forward.

"I'll ask the manager," she said, disappearing through the large kitchen door.

A few minutes passed before she came back to the main area of the Cracker Barrel Store, where I stood

"I THINK THEY WILL"

looking at all the toys and candy.

"My manager said the best way is to take all the orders, tally up the total and give you the check," she said, looking straight into my eyes

"That's perfect," I replied.

Other employees must have overheard her discuss my request with her boss because every waitress that came out of the kitchen delivering breakfast orders looked at me and smiled.

When Makallah handed me the ticket she was full of emotion and so was I. Maybe her grandfather does things like this for others or maybe she doesn't have a grandfather anymore. I don't know, but I know she was dear. I accepted the check.

She stood there looking up at me wanting to say something, but wasn't ready to say anything.

"I'm eighty," I said with a raspy voice and tears welling up. "When I get old I hope someone will buy me a breakfast."

Touching my own weathered and wrinkled right arm so very gently she said, "I think they will."

Rpj

July 4th 2013

He really is in Charge

THE ATTENTION SPAN of most fellow senior citizens for listening to a sermon is around five minutes of rapt attention, followed by five minutes of some attention, and maybe another five minutes hit and miss if a concerted effort is made to listen hard. After that, I usually start counting how brick courses around the windows and doors or determining how many times fish are depicted in the stained glass windows surrounding the main part of Blessed Sacrament church ... or just drifting off to think about my own problems.

I went to Google.com this evening and found about 250,000 articles on attention span and what a problem it is for church-goers, especially when preachers and pastors feel they have the skill to hold a congregation in rapture for an hour.

I write this because we have a new priest at Blessed Sacrament. He's young, nice-looking, eloquent, and likes to sing as much of the mass as possible. His name is Father

HE REALLY IS IN CHARGE

Schamber, and he challenges the congregation to respond with vigor and on key to his voice. He has given long sermons without realizing that many parishioners' eyes were glazed over and their minds had been transported to faraway places, or maybe just wondering if they were going to have to wait in line very long at the Golden Corral buffet for the "blue hair special" of the day.

I had trouble singing Gregorian Latin phrases in English, particularly at 8:00 a.m. mass. I also had trouble with the length of his sermons. It's my problem, however, because the young priest is eager, intelligent, devout, and full of faith. So, I had to figure out a way to cope.

On Sundays, when the cantor announced that another priest, besides Father Schamber would say mass, I smiled and felt like I had dodged a bullet. But that's the wrong attitude, so I made up my mind to realize the church is the people, and every priest isn't going to conduct Mass the way I want. After all, he is trying to push me toward salvation. So, I had some guilt about my selfish, misguided feelings.

Mindy and I left for church, while Gary and Jean and little Stephen were leaving for Banner Elk, North Carolina. We drove to Blessed Sacrament. The parking angel found a convenient parking place for us – always a plus. We decided to sit on the right side of the church and selected aisle seats, said our prayers, and got our minds prepared for Mass. I should mention that Mindy had agreed to substitute for a friend in the Perpetual Adoration program and was to be in the chapel from 11:00 a.m. until noon.

Just before the bell rang at the rear door of the church signaling the start of Mass, the cantor asked us to rise and welcome Father Schamber. I looked at Mindy and rolled my eyes, knowing that a singing ritual would soon start, followed by a very long sermon.

I tried to make myself accept things as they were, but I still didn't sing the responses. I only said them. The first reading was long, as was the gospel, but both were very interesting and familiar. Time came for the sermon to begin, and Father Schamber took his notes out and delivered a very good sermon. He challenged us to support Bishop Ricard's vision to put things in place in the diocese. It took less than fifteen minutes and it looked like he had the congregation's attention the whole time. When Mass was over we went home for a little while.

We took care of some chores, and then headed back to the chapel at about 10:35 p.m. We found a parking space again, even though 10:30 Mass was already under way. Mindy signed us in on the Perpetual Adoration timesheet. We picked up a religious periodical from the book rack and sat down in our seats for what always seemed like the quickest hour in the world. We heard the congregation singing a beautiful hymn just on the other side of the chapel wall.

HE REALLY IS IN CHARGE

Then we heard Father Schamber sing in a loud and melodic chant, "The Lord be with you," to which the congregation responded, "And with your spirit."

Mindy and I looked at each other. Not only was it out of the norm for Father Schamber to say the 8:00 a.m. and 10:30 a.m. Masses, but there we were in the chapel, filling in for someone else, when the Lord wanted to make sure we got a full dose of Father Schamber that day.

We smiled at each other, said "Thank you, Jesus." Then we settled in and listened to the rest of the 10:30 Mass and the beautiful singing of Father Schamber, the choir, and the congregation.

He really is in charge.

A Moment of Spiritual Enchantment

THE HOLY SPIRIT'S presence is often felt by people lucky enough to have faith and be in a place conducive to shutting off the daily trials and tribulations of life. On numerous occasions during my eighty-four years on earth, I've been overwhelmed by the presence of a Great Power gently touching me.

Blessed Sacrament church sits among the rolling hills near downtown Tallahassee. The brick building has massive laminated wood beams holding up an expansive paneled roof. Above the altar and on both sides of it are modernistic stained glass panels depicting Jesus in various scenes from his short time on earth as a man. The larger panel directly above the altar shows Jesus and the twelve disciples at the Last Supper. The subtle component of the stained glass panel shows that one of the disciples has turned away from the Lord. It's a very comfortable

A MOMENT OF SPIRITUAL ENCHANTMENT

place of worship, especially when the guardian of the air conditioner control box turns it on to cool the church.

The congregation is as diverse as America. That's why I enjoy it so much. The parish community is composed of all races and all ages, from newborn babies to seniors. They represent the entire range of economic strata. It has officials from the highest judicial bench to part-time laborers and everything in between. Blessed Sacrament parish reflects the best of what the Catholic Church and America offers its people.

My wife of sixty-three years and I have been members of the parish since 1964. We've always been blessed with at least one Irish priest. Monsignor O'Sullivan is a most devout man and brings honor to his special calling. Our pastor is a very holy man.

There are certain songs sung during our liturgy that always cause chills and, at the same time, warm emotions deep within my soul. When our closing hymn is "God Bless America," I swell with pride and give thanks for my God, my family and my country. It's refreshing to rejuvenate my soul with beautiful music, people of similar faith, and the opportunity to observe life and all of its challenges so gracefully reflected in the faces and voices of the congregation.

I was saying the Creed during the 10:30 a.m. Mass one Sunday and glanced to my right to see a middle-aged lady using sign language for the four young children seated with her, and I assume, her husband. A young Asian girl, who must be part of that family, was watching every trance-inducing move of the lady's hands. The girl appeared to be twelve years old or so, and was flawlessly repeating every hand-sign communicated by the fast-moving hands of her teacher. I watched the young girl silently while praying the Creed and thought of all of my grandchildren and children. How lucky they are to be blessed with such good health. My heart beat faster, and tears welled up. I could no longer speak out loud. I couldn't take my eyes off that sweet act of love that God was allowing me to witness.

I learned many years ago that the Holy Spirit moves in mysterious ways. I feel so fortunate to be spiritually enchanted, and I pray I never lose that gift.

Unbeknownst to me, that was indeed a special family – so special, in fact, that a network television program built a new house for them in Tallahassee. The husband died while the new house was under construction, but he knew his family was going to be taken care of. How dear was that?

Ever Think You Are in Charge?

I LEFT ON a whirlwind tour yesterday morning for lunch with Lessie and John at noon in Jacksonville, and then to a 2:00 funeral at the St. Augustine Cathedral for Sal Versaggi's Aunt Pat. Malinda and I used to play cards with her and Manny Versaggi when they visited their St. Augustine beach house during the summer in the 1960s. Manny always pulled a beach seine in the shallow waters for mullet and whiting and always cooked fennel sausage on his little grill on the beach when the 5:00 p.m. libations were served. The delicious sausages were made for him in Tampa.

Those were special times and special people. After Communion I walked to my car parked near the seawall and swiftly headed for a 4:30 p.m. interview with Rodney and Mary Jean Thompson at their house in Titusville.

After the interview, the Thompson family and I drove to Dixie Crossroads for fresh shrimp and fish. The waitress brought out a plate of appetizers consisting of fried oysters, fried mullet fillets, and fried coconut shrimp on a platter big enough for a party of 20. We were only seven. That's what happens when you go to a restaurant with the owner.

After the appetizer feast I ordered a small piece of broiled pompano, coleslaw (Momma always said to eat a vegetable), and a liter of unsweetened tea. I still had thirty miles to go after dinner to get to my motel, so I finally crawled into a hard bed at 9:35 p.m. The small case of indigestion got under way about that same time (I forgot to take my pill).

I woke up and looked at the clock, which said 6:42, so I got up. When I looked at my watch while brushing my teeth, it said 5:55. Somebody forgot to fall back with the clocks, so I was not happy. But after my 8:00 a.m. appointment, I headed to Tallahassee.

When I got to Daytona Beach, I thought about giving my grandson, Tad Mask, a call to see if he could drive out to I-95 and meet me for lunch. When he answered the phone, he was on I-95, probably six or seven miles from me. So, we decided to get off at Exit 261 and go to the Cracker Barrel for lunch.

It was wonderful talking to this bright young man, hearing his plans, and exchanging political views. I didn't have a lot of cash since Mindy only gives me a small allowance (just, kidding, Mindy), so I slipped him a few dollars like I usually do when I get the chance. I figured

EVER THINK YOU ARE IN CHARGE?

I didn't need more than $20 to get home because I had a credit card.

There was a lot of traffic on the road until I got to I-10 in Jacksonville and then moved quickly to my normal stopping place at Highway 129. People often stand at the stop sign there looking for a ride or some money. Long ago, Mindy and I decided to always be willing to buy someone a sandwich and a drink just to make sure they had some food.

This particular day, I turned on the exit ramp to get off I-10 and I noticed a figure standing near the stop sign. I hoped I had enough money to get him a sandwich and still get me a Diet Coke and some cheese crackers. As I approached the stop sign, I saw a little mutt prancing around at the feet of a girl. The young lady was wearing rimless glasses and dressed in ragged clothes of many dark colors and a brown knit hat. She was holding a sign from the top of a cardboard box that said,

"I'm ugly, and I'm broke."

I got a lump in my throat. I rolled my window down and stopped at the sign and asked her if she'd like a sandwich and Coke.

"I would, thank you," she said in a low voice.

"I'll be right back," I replied as I rolled up the window and turned left.

I drove to the Shell station, filled the car with gas, and went inside to find the largest sandwich I could and a big bottle of Coke. I was able to put the goods on my Amex and slipped my $10 bill inside the bag. I was having trouble keeping myself composed, so I hurried back to the car, sat quietly in the seat for a few seconds, and drove back to the place where the young girl was waiting.

When I got there, she was sitting on the grass with her little dog snuggled next to her. She walked over to the window, and that's when I saw her lovely, young face that reminded me of my children and grandchildren. I handed her the bag and could barely speak any words, but I said, "Honey, lemme tell you something. You are not ugly, and you are not totally broke anymore."

She gently took the bag and looked directly at me and said,

"Thank you so very much."

"No," I said, "thank you very much, and may God bless you."

I was sobbing before I pulled back on I-10 and couldn't completely stop for about fifteen miles or so. When I thought about that young face a few more times on the way home, I choked up and sobbed again. There, but for the grace of God go my children and grandchildren.

Mindy and I went to several different Masses last week, and each time, the Gospel pertaining to the Final Judgment (Matthew 25) came up. It was also read at the funeral service yesterday. The message is ingrained in my heart, my mind, and my soul. "Whatsoever you do for the

EVER THINK YOU ARE IN CHARGE?

least of My children, that you do unto Me." I believe that.

I called Mindy to tell her about my joyfully sad moment. I could hardly speak but I managed to say to her, "I hope the Holy Spirit knows I've only got five dollars left in case He sends me another opportunity."

We chuckled together.

I didn't write this to brag about a random act of kindness. I wrote it to show that we are not in charge and that the Holy Spirit moves in mysterious and wonderful ways.

My Special Board of Memories

IF YOU LOOK real close at the art board hanging above my work table you will see it was created on May 15, 2003.

We lived at 2147 Pink Flamingo Drive, and I just began building bird houses. I used two coats of bright yellow latex paint for a base coat on the board early one Saturday morning. Cindy said she was coming by to teach me how to paint birds, trees, and flowers for the eclectic assortment of my unfinished bird houses on a shelf in the garage.

Cindy arrived after lunch, and Mindy joined us as we opened up a set of variable use brushes of many designs.

MY SPECIAL BOARD OF MEMORIES

Cindy brought them as a gift to get her daddy started out on the right foot with the proper supplies. She brought lots of little bottles of paint in all colors and shades and showed me how to place the paint on a palette or paper plate so that I could add different colors to create the shade I desired.

One of the first things Cindy drew was a funny looking backwards "S" and a backwards "4" as the legs for the bird. Then she started drawing a flamingo, which you will notice near the far right next to the backward "S." If you look above her flamingo, you will see the one I painted. As someone who is seriously art-challenged, you will quickly notice on my flamingo that the beak is pointed up instead of down, but that's where the image in my mind made my brush go. The two very small flamingos near the outer branch of the lower tree were painted by Mindy, who has a much better touch than me.

I did a credible job with the big tree and the huge branch coming in from the left side. One of my trees looks like it was painted upside down, though, but we actually turned the board around to find some space.

The big smiling face of the elderly gentleman on the left side of the picture was created 85 years ago. I keep this very special piece of board over my work bench table because it makes me smile and evokes wonderful sets of memories of our family to retrieve whenever I wish.

Everyone ought to have a special board of memories.

Speaking of My Mortality

DYING IS A subject Mindy prefers to avoid. Not that she is unaware of the inevitable – it's just that she prefers to talk and think about other things. I respect her for that and try not to burden her with my off-the-wall thoughts and comments.

But for me, Bobby Jones, I accept the fact that I won't climb Mt. Everest or even a small pyramid again. I won't go offshore fishing with the enthusiasm and strength I had two decades ago. I won't dance or love as often, but when I do dance or love, it will be just as joyful as it has always been. I accept that I will lose long-time beloved family and friends, and one day, my allotted time will be over.

Those who love me will accept the true circle of life. If they are as wise as I think they are, they will understand and appreciate what has gone on before them. They, like many of us who have been through the closing of life, will come out the other side of grief as wiser and more sensitive persons.

SPEAKING OF MY MORTALITY

Our day is hidden from us. This is good from one perspective, but not so good from another. Not knowing when my day will come gives me strength to persevere – to continue fighting the bad and working for the good. Not knowing continues the myth that I will live forever, but that is not so, of course.

On the other hand, if I knew when my hour was coming, I could get things together. I could tell my family and friends goodbye and tell them that I love them. I could sit down in a quiet spot with my family and look them all in the eyes, saying how proud I am of all of them and how deeply I have loved them all their lives. I would assure them I will go to a better place where you don't get old and suffer the pains of aging. I would ask for their patience, understanding, and love as the life process shuts down. Most of all, I could look into those amazing brown eyes of Mindy – who is the best thing that ever happened to me – and thank God for her love, support, and respect. If someone asked me what I would like carved on my grave stone, I would be at peace if it said, "Bobby Jones sure did love Malinda Usina."

Also by
ROBERT P. JONES

A Culture Worth Saving

Florida and fishing have been synonymous since Admiral Pedro Menéndez de Avilés founded St. Augustine in 1565. He brought myriad tradesmen, including net makers and fishermen who harvested seafood for sustenance and trade. From 1880 through 1925, four million Italian immigrants arrived in the United States, along with immigrants from Spain, Portugal, Ireland, Scotland, and Scandinavia. Thousands of families migrated to Florida, searching for economic and political freedom. Thankfully, many chose commercial fishing.

Florida's fishing industry has long been a melting pot of diverse languages, customs, and characters. Robert P. Jones, a modern-day gunslinger for commercial fishing for nearly 50 years, has compiled a comprehensive and fascinating book about the people who created the Florida commercial fishing culture—a culture he has dedicated his career to saving.

Learn more at:
www.outskirtspress.com/acultureworthsaving

Also by
ROBERT P. JONES

Death at the Inlet
Freedom is not free

Felton Ponce enjoyed a carefree childhood in St. Augustine when it was just a small Florida coastal town, long before it was rediscovered by northerners and tourists from all over the world. He spent countless afternoons as a youngster watching the shrimpers and red snapper fishermen on the unloading dock at Salvadora's Seafood Market—and by the time he was in the sixth grade, he was hooked for life. Years later, as a commercial fisherman, Felton finds himself face-to-face with a terrorist plot to kill thousands of innocent Americans. Government agents step in to try and stop the terrorists, but they'll need all the help they can get from the local fishermen if they are to protect the public from a deadly poison. Death at the Inlet is a riveting adventure that will leave you wondering about the vulnerability of our country's food supply.

Learn more at:
www.outskirtspress.com/DeathattheInlet

CPSIA information can be obtained
at www.ICGtesting.com
Printed in the USA
FFOW03n0117190318
45817953-46720FF